STO

D1094612

JUL 27 '72

WHO'S WATCHING THE AIRWAYS?

WHO'S WATCHING THE AIRWAYS?

The Dangerous Games of the FAA

PHILIP I. RYTHER
as told to STEPHEN M. AUG

DOUBLEDAY & COMPANY, INC., GARDEN CITY, NEW YORK, 1972

Library of Congress Catalog Card Number 78–186658
Copyright © 1972 by Philip I. Ryther & Stephen M. Aug
All Rights Reserved
Printed in the United States of America
First Edition

This book is dedicated to the more than fifty thousand employees of the Federal Aviation Administration. These men and women represent a world of experience in aviation. In my more than twelve years working with them—and as one of them—I found them to be conscientious and possessed of unquestioned integrity and loyalty not only to the government, but to the American people generally.

1681673

FOREWORD

It seems to me that the American people not only have a right to know, but want to learn just how their federal bureaucracy really operates, and the manner in which their affairs are being handled—and mishandled—by their government. This book deals with one facet of that bureaucracy, the Federal Aviation Administration, whose leadership founders in inefficiency, cooperates inordinately with the industry it was established to regulate, and neglects the welfare of millions of passengers. It was in the FAA that I worked for twelve years starting in 1959 and ending on December 31, 1970, when I was hounded out of the agency for my repeated attempts to bring about important reforms.

From the outset of my tenure at the FAA, I was continually amazed at the talent, knowledge, skill and dedication of 99 percent of the employees of the agency. In fact, I can truthfully say that their dedication to their work—protecting the lives and property of those

who fly in our nation's aircraft—ranks among the highest
of any organization with which I have become acquainted. But it is because of the other less than 1 percent who are so imbued with their own self-interest and
so concerned with political in-fighting to get to the top
of the bureaucracy that the FAA's truly dedicated staff
of professionals is, in effect, performing without leadership—at least the kind of leadership that this agency and
the nation so desperately need.

This book presents a case-by-case indictment of the top
management of the FAA. Much of the material is gath-
ered from still-secret FAA reports and from letters and
other internal documents. All of the incidents in this
book are true. All can be documented. Together they
show that through its incredibly poor management the
FAA has failed to afford the American public the protection it so badly needs in the field of aviation safety.

If nothing else, this book is a demand for a sweeping
overhaul of the management of the Federal Aviation Administration.

Philip I. Ryther

McLean, Virginia

CONTENTS

WHO'S WATCHING THE AIRWAYS?

CHAPTER I

LIMITED VISION

The sky was clear blue that morning—October 2, 1970—
and the seventy-one young passengers peering through
the plane windows could see the sharp, jagged line of
mountains just to the west as their two twin-engine
Martin 404's swept in for a landing at Denver's Stapleton
Field.

The planes, owned by an Oklahoma City firm, had
been chartered under a bizarre arrangement to Wichita
State University and were operated by a second Okla-
homa City firm for the purpose of flying the Wichita
State University football team from Wichita, Kansas, to
Logan, Utah, to play Utah State University.

The stop in Denver was for refueling, but Ronald G.
Skipper, president of Golden Eagle Aviation Inc., which
supplied the flight crews for the two planes, used the
time on the ground as a chance to buy some additional
charts. He was going to give his passengers a little some-

thing extra on this flight—a scenic trip over the central Colorado Rockies.

The scenic route wasn't in the original flight plan for either of the two planes, but Skipper was determined. Besides, it wouldn't take any longer and it would make the flight more interesting. At least that's what he told his passengers as he chatted with them for about fifteen minutes before his plane took off for Logan. The fifteen minutes of chatter may well have been one of Skipper's fatal mistakes. The original flight plan called for both planes to fly north from Denver over the high plains east of the mountains, allowing the heavily loaded craft plenty of time to gain altitude before they made their westward swing over the Rockies, somewhere around Laramie, Wyoming.

Skipper made the decision to take the scenic route, however, after the two planes left Wichita that morning. He made the decision, he said, without the benefit of any advice from Danny Crocker, the pilot of the plane—and, supposedly, the man in charge of the craft. It was, though, an awkward situation. While Crocker was pilot, he was actually working for his copilot, Skipper. Crocker was employed as a mechanic at Golden Eagle, but occasionally, as in this case, was used as a pilot.

Just how he became aware of the plan to fly the scenic route through the mountains never has been made clear. He could have learned of it through casual conversation with Skipper during the flight from Wichita, or he could have learned about it from Leland Everett, pilot of the other 404 as they talked on the ground during the seventy-minute stopover at Denver.

The two planes left Stapleton Field about half past

noon—with Everett's craft and its thirty-five passengers heading on the originally planned northern route, and Skipper's on its ill-fated scenic trip over the Rockies.

Skipper had had no specific conversation with Captain Crocker concerning the scenic route and, as Skipper later said, there was no flight planning other than his informal intention "to go to Logan direct—or as direct as possible." Somewhat north of Denver, Skipper's plane turned west and headed into the mountains. According to witnesses on the ground, the plane passed just west of Idaho Springs, a small community in the heart of what was at one time Colorado's booming gold and silver mining country.

Skipper eventually spotted Clear Creek and U. S. Highway 6, which runs alongside it through Clear Creek Valley. He began following the highway as it wound through the mountains past Georgetown and Silver Plume on the way toward Loveland Pass, at 11,990 feet the highest year-round major highway in the nation. The sight of a big aircraft snaking its way through the canyon perhaps five hundred or one thousand feet above the canyon floor —in a canyon flanked by thirteen-thousand-foot-plus mountains—was sufficiently curious to attract a few spectators on the ground below.

One of these, an engineer for the Martin Marietta Corporation—himself a former bomber pilot—recalled later that he was "awed by the aspect of such a large aircraft cruising up the valley." But he also recalled something just as strange—the engines didn't seem to be running with enough power to clear the Continental Divide which lay just ahead, but beyond Skipper's line of sight.

"When the plane made a turn to the right," he remembered, "I noticed a mushiness to its flight characteristics. Both engines appeared to be running normally, no smoke, fire or sounds of missing or backfiring."

Another witness on the ground, a pilot familiar with the Loveland Pass area, was driving toward Denver on U.S. 6 and was about two miles east of a place called Dry Gulch when he saw the plane. He said, "Thinking it must be in trouble, I stopped the car to get out and look and listen.

"My initial and firm feeling was that the plane was in serious trouble as it was below the level of the mountains on either side that form the valley, and I didn't see how it could possibly turn around.

"Also, it was in nose-high attitude, but barely keeping up with the rise of terrain. I have driven over this route countless times and know that the steepness of the slope increases radically in only three or four miles from where he was and that the plane could never make it."

This horrifying possibility apparently didn't occur to Skipper as he flew along the canyon, catching glimpses of occasional snowy peaks in the distance and of glistening yellow aspen trees in among the dense green of the mountain foliage.

He had spent his last minutes on the ground in Denver chatting with the passengers—was it about the following day's football game at Utah State? Or was he telling them about the rugged scenery of the central Colorado Rockies that they were about to see? Had he spent those valuable minutes examining his newly purchased charts, he would have noticed that while the elevation of the canyon floor at Georgetown is 8,512 feet above sea level, the floor rises to 9,118 at Silver Plume and 10,600 feet at the Loveland ski resort area, ending at an altitude of 12,700 feet at the

Continental Divide. In the area west of Georgetown, the mountains on either side of Clear Creek Valley range from 12,477 feet to more than 13,000 feet, and the pilot of a plane proceeding west along the valley at an altitude of 11,000 feet or less would not be able to see the end of the valley until reaching Dry Gulch, since it would be cut off from view by 13,234-foot-high Mount Sniktau.

"We were in the valley," Skipper recalled later. "It began to look to me as if we were not going to climb so as to have clearance—sufficient clearance—over what I now know to be the Continental Divide ahead of us.

"I said something to the effect to Captain Crocker that maybe we should reverse course and gain some altitude.

"I initiated a turn to the right. We were on the left side slightly of the valley. . . . I initiated a turn of approximately 45 degrees change in heading, a medium bank turn which in my mind is somewhere between 20 and 30 degrees.

"And as I was rolling out of this turn, Captain Crocker said, 'I've got the airplane.' He initiated a left turn, the aircraft began vibrating, he put the nose down and shortly thereafter we crashed."

What had happened, the National Transportation Safety Board later determined, was that in their terror at finding themselves in a box canyon, Skipper and Crocker poured on the power in order to make a sharp left turn and the engines—which had been operating at the bare minimum to maintain control—stalled under the sudden heavy load. The plane plunged into a heavily wooded mountainside.

Glenn Kostal, starting right linebacker for the Wichita Shockers, had been at the rear of the plane chatting with four teammates when he realized something was wrong. He recalled much of it vividly, especially the crash: "The impact ripped the side of the plane wide open and then I heard an explosion," he said.

The next thing Kostal realized, blood was gushing from a gash on his forehead. He was so stunned, he didn't fully realize what had happened. "I saw the hole and heard people telling me to get up. There was dirt and smoke all around. It seemed like the whole side and bottom of the plane had ripped out. We could hear quite a few screams inside. A couple of guys went back to the plane to try to get some of the other players out, but they couldn't do it."

Apparently, there were a number of survivors of the crash who had not made it out of the plane when it burst into flame. They were burned to death. Skipper, who himself was seriously injured, recalled seeing and talking with passengers lying in the forward baggage compartment. He could see them through the partly open cockpit door, but the opening was too small to reach them. Some of the first rescue workers who climbed the mountainside from a nearby highway recalled also seeing passengers on the floor making no effort to extricate themselves. But before rescuers could enter the plane, there was an explosion, and flames engulfed the craft.

Rescuers later found things such as battered black-and-gold football helmets scattered along the ground, with smoldering shirts and ties, shoulder pads, a charred book of football plays and a pair of cleated shoes with No. 63 marked inside. Dead were Crocker, a stewardess, Kansas State legislator Ray King, Coach Ben Wilson and his wife, Athletic Director A. C. (Bert) Williams and his wife, and thirteen football players. Thirty persons died in the crash or later in hospitals. Nine passengers and one crew member—Skipper—were injured, but survived.

The National Transportation Safety Board, which investigates major disasters involving airplanes, trains, vessels, automobiles and pipelines, confirmed that the probable cause of the accident had been the "intentional operation of the aircraft over a mountain valley route at an altitude from which the aircraft could neither climb over the obstructing terrain ahead, nor execute a successful course reversal." Their report said that significant factors included the overloaded condition of the plane, "the virtual absence of flight planning for the chosen route of the flight from Denver to Logan, a lack of understanding on the part of the crew of the performance capabilities and limitations of the aircraft, and the lack of operational management to monitor and appropriately control the actions of the flight crew."

Strangely, though, the safety board placed much of the blame for the wreck on the weird leasing arrangement. In the wake of the crash, nobody wanted to acknowledge responsibility for the plane or the flight. Who would pay the survivors' medical costs? Who would be the defendant in the lawsuits which would result from such a tragedy? The Federal Aviation Administration said Golden Eagle Aviation, which had supplied the crew, was the operator. But both Golden Eagle and Jack Richards Aircraft Co., which owned the plane, contended that Wichita State University was really the operator. Wichita State said it had merely chartered the service, and that it was really Jack Richards and Golden Eagle who must share the blame.

The safety board declined to enter this part of the matter, considering its duty to have been completed. The board did conclude, however, that "the numerous deficiencies, unsafe practices, and deviations from regulations involved in this operation are typical of operations where none of the participants acknowledge responsibility for the safe conduct of a flight. . . . The board believes that the management required for a safe operation appears to have been absent and was a significant factor in this accident."

The crash produced the usual furor that results from a major disaster. A week after the tragedy, Secretary of Transportation John A. Volpe ordered a detailed investigation of companies designated as "commercial operators of large aircraft." The difference between these so-called "commercial operators" and scheduled airlines is important. A scheduled airline must have a certificate of public convenience and necessity from the Civil Aeronautics Board in order to fly regularly over a specified route. In addition, it must have an FAA certificate, which it can obtain only if it has a qualified crew, training program, and proper management. It must also meet the stringent requirements of Federal Aviation Regulation 121 governing crew training and proficiency, maintenance practices, quality control and terminal facilities. By contrast, a "commercial operator" needs no CAB certificate since he flies only irregularly and hires out his services to carry people or freight anywhere they want to go at any time. He operates under Federal Aviation Regulation 91 which says, in effect, fly safely. It has no requirements for crew training, mechanical or maintenance standards or quality control.

To conduct the investigation, Volpe appointed Willard

J. Smith an assistant secretary of transportation for safety and consumer affairs. Smith, a Coast Guard admiral who had recently retired as commandant of the Coast Guard, had been a pilot more than thirty years. At the same time, Federal Aviation Administrator John H. Shaffer announced that the licenses of both Jack Richards and Golden Eagle had been revoked. Shaffer contended their business arrangement was a "façade" to duck air safety regulations.

Twenty-five days after the accident, and still grasping for something—anything that would give the appearance at least that the government was actually trying to prevent similar disasters in the future—Volpe announced a proposed FAA regulation which he said would broaden safety rules applicable to the operation of large aircraft leased to colleges, universities and other educational institutions. The regulation—which was quietly dropped a year later after the Wichita furor had died down—would have made these charters subject to the same safety rules as apply to air travel clubs when using aircraft weighing more than 12,500 pounds for carrying groups such as students, athletic teams and choral groups.

At the same time, the FAA—which is part of the Department of Transportation—announced it was going to redefine the term "commercial operator" to expressly include aircraft operations conducted by persons hauling cargo or goods for the purpose of reselling it themselves, as well as operations conducted for such business as the sale of real estate, hotel accommodations or other property.

This new definition was intended to correct misunderstanding which existed about whether or not an airplane

operation was "for compensation or hire." Under FAA
regulations a commercial operator is a person who "for
compensation or hire, engages in the carriage by aircraft
in air commerce of persons or property other than as an
air carrier. . . . When it is doubtful that an operation is
for 'compensation or for hire,' the test applied is whether
the carriage by air is merely incidental to the person's
other business or is, in itself, a major enterprise for profit."

The purpose of this legal definition is to provide that
an educational institution renting a plane without a crew
—and obtaining pilot services separately—would have im-
posed upon it operational and maintenance requirements
similar to those for regular airlines. This, presumably,
would eliminate the considerable confusion in connection
with the Wichita State crash over who had ultimate responsibility for the flight—the school would.

No other action was taken until, in March 1971—five
months after the crash—Admiral Smith's task force reported. Its principal conclusion was that technology was
changing, and bigger, more complex planes that had
been used by the airlines were coming into the hands of
charter operators and therefore "the federal regulatory
scheme must be re-examined and needed changes made."

To track down these dangerous charter operations and
make the public aware of them, Admiral Smith recommended that an intensive FAA surveillance program that
was conducted in November and December 1970 be re-
instituted because it was "a real deterrent to 'illegal'
charter operations." (The FAA, in commenting on the
recommendations, said it liked the idea, but it couldn't
afford the manpower.) An educational flyer, he suggested, should be developed on the hazards in the leasing

or chartering of large planes under the then present regulations. (The FAA agreed but said it would have its own Flight Standards Service and its press agents make up the proper folder.) And the government should take an additional education measure: a "Truth in Leasing" clause should be added to leases of large or complex planes to alert the unwary to the operator responsibilities in which it would be involving itself. (The FAA agreed with his recommendation but, in the best tradition of federal regulatory agencies, it wasn't certain it had the legal authority to add a clause to help the consumer, and it noted that a new rule was pending.)

As to the flights themselves, Smith said the FAA should "as quickly as possible" require all large or complex airplanes to be operated on a flight plan at all times—except for local test flights and ferry flights which take empty planes from airport to airport. (The FAA agreed this would help track down illegal charter operators, but it said it would have to study the matter because of its possible impact on the air traffic control system.) New rules should be issued to provide that all large and complex planes operated in charter service be maintained and operated at a level of safety comparable to airplanes of regular certificated operators—but without the detailed administrative, financial and organizational requirements of the large operators. (The FAA, in answer, pointed to one recent amendment to its rules, a proposed rule, and a proposal to issue a rule that might be in this area.) After an evaluation period to assure that the level of safety of the charter carriers has been brought up to par with certificated carriers, Smith advised that action be taken to eliminate the requirement of certification of operators who engage only in private carriage—in effect, those who don't carry any paying passengers. (FAA said this recommendation should be directed at the Civil Aeronautics Board, which regulates the economics of the aviation industry, as FAA regulates safety.

To plan for the future, Smith proposed that a study be initiated to determine the extent of public need for operating large, complex airplanes privately for hire. (The FAA considered this, too, a CAB matter and added that "the mere fact that illegal operations are so extensive indicates an economic need that is not now under the cognizance of the Civil Aeronautics Board," and much of the charter business going to illegal operators is that which regular and supplemental airlines either cannot or will not handle.)

Admiral Smith's recommendations, sound as they are, actually touch only a very small portion of the safety problems of U.S. civil aviation. Further, as we have seen, they were made in response to a tragedy and therefore they are a response only to the issues that it raised.

The Wichita State wreck, however, needn't have happened, because for six months prior to the crash, the FAA had had available to it a complete evaluation of its own flight standards programs—an evaluation that told the FAA where its safety problems were most acute, and how they might be cured. The report was the work of a team of six FAA evaluators—directed by me—who were very much like an army inspector general's staff.

In preparing our report, we visited every segment of aviation in this nation: airlines, pilots, training organizations, maintenance crews. We met with innumerable officials of flying schools and mechanic schools, and with any number of air base operators. We spoke with aviation officials of a dozen states. We met with dozens upon dozens of our own field inspectors who really are the eyes and ears of the FAA; we met with a wide cross section of the home office of the FAA who were involved in safety. We talked with 210 groups of people—more than seven hundred individuals—in the course of that five-month investigation. And we traveled more than 150,000 miles.

By the time we'd finished, we had three filing cabinets full of materials—all of which we condensed into eight general subjects and thirty recommendations in a twenty-nine-page report. Significantly, our report contained two recommendations which, had they been adopted, might have prevented the Wichita State crash: one to upgrade the regulations governing "noncertificated" operators to provide stricter controls over all phases of their operations, and a second to intensify surveillance and enforcement to keep pace with the growing charter segment of aviation.

If the FAA had taken a warning in our report, the bizarre leasing agreement involving Wichita State and the obvious lack of advance planning for that trip over the mountains would have been prevented: "Many [FAA] inspectors are concerned over their inability to properly control or surveil [sic] the activities of noncertified aircraft operators. These operators engage in the commercial transportation of passengers and cargo under the very minimal requirements of FAR Part 91 [Federal Aviation Regulations Part 91 governs private planes, and its provisions are far more lenient than the safety rules of Part 121 for regular commercial planes]. Qualifications of crews and mechanics employed by many of these operators are marginal, and inspectors, in an attempt to improve the safety of these operators, often devote an inordinate amount of time to this surveillance. Some inspectors have resorted to appealing to the better judgment of 'customers' in attempting to dissuade them from doing business with operators who they feel operate in a potentially hazardous manner."

This report—which contained far more recommendations than those dealing simply with charter operations—was completed March 30, 1970. From then until I was hounded out of the FAA at the end of 1970 I tried time after time to convince agency officials to implement the reforms which our evaluators pointed out were clearly needed. Not only did I fail to obtain any action, but my efforts were seen as an attempt to override my superiors in one of the most oppressive bureaucracies in the federal government. One of my superiors, a deputy administrator, even wrote, after seeing the report and listening to me present it orally at an hour-and-a-half briefing for several senior FAA officials, that he "was not convinced that your report was sufficiently urgent to justify bypassing the normal management channels and procedures of coordination in presenting your findings."

Just four months later twenty-eight persons were killed on a Colorado mountainside in one accident alone and two died later in hospitals. In all, 1,270 persons died in 1970 in general aviation accidents, most of them involving small planes.

And although our report warned clearly and concisely of the dangers of these phony leasing operators, the incredible truth is that the FAA had had some clear indications of what was going on as early as 1965. It was during the summer of that year that the FAA launched an investigation of illegal commercial flights in the Miami, Florida, and San Juan, Puerto Rico, areas. A report of that investigation—still labeled FOR OFFICIAL USE ONLY—contains this clear statement of just what was happening:

"Of the potentially large volume of unlawful operators detected, many used the subterfuge lease as a means of avoiding immediate detection. A great deal of confusion reigns in the area of what can and cannot be done in the transportation of passengers and cargo in large aircraft.

"The confusion is related primarily to factual applications to the existing law rather than to the law itself. The law seems clear that no person shall operate an aircraft, large or small, carrying passengers or property for compensation or hire without an air carrier, commercial operator or ATCO [air transport commercial operator] certificate.

"The difficulty revolves about the determination of when a legitimate leasing agreement affects the transfer of operational control of an aircraft to the lessee. The most efficient means of identifying a legitimate lessee is to determine the intent of the parties to the written agreement.

"Quite often, when one wishes to take advantage of a low price offered by an uncertificated operator, he may initially cooperate in the execution of a sham lease. However, when he is asked if he intends to assume the responsibility for the maintenance of the aircraft and the selection, training, and instruction of the crew with all that implies, he confesses the illegitimacy of the lease."

That investigation, performed by John J. Keyser, a special trial counsel, and Joseph T. Hornsby, a special assistant in the Flight Standards Service, recommended among other things that regulations governing large aviation aircraft be elevated to impose, with some relaxation, the standards of maintenance and operations required for regulation commercial planes. It recommended also that all pilots in command of large aircraft have the minimum of proficiency and flight time required of airline transport pilots; that they be rated for the type of plane they are flying; that they be subject to flight time limitations and be required to successfully complete at least annually, if not semiannually, proficiency checks much like those required of all airline flight crew members, which would be preceded by recurrent training.

That report was dated December 8, 1965—nearly five years before the Wichita crash. The recommendations obviously were never put into effect.

Slightly more than a month after the Wichita tragedy —on the night of November 14, 1970—another chartered airliner crash shocked the nation. This time a plane chartered from Southern Airways and carrying members of the Marshall University football team back to Huntington, West Virginia, smashed into a ridge about a mile from the end of the runway at Tri-State Airport near Huntington. Seventy-five persons were killed in that wreck which, at this writing, still is under investigation by the National Transportation Safety Board.

The Huntington wreck was in some respects vastly different from that of the Wichita crash. For one thing, the plane was operated by a regular airline and flown by an experienced pilot. However, under charter regulations, there is no requirement that a pilot must have flown into a given airport before he is permitted to carry passengers there. There is such an FAA requirement for regular commercial flights. In this case, Captain Frank Abbott, one of Southern's senior pilots, had never before flown to Tri-State.

Tri-State had only half the radio guidance system used for instrument landings. Instrument landing system (ILS) runways normally have two special radio beams along the approach path, one to guide planes horizontally as they line up with the runway, and another to guide them vertically as they descend to the proper touchdown spot. Tri-State had the horizontal localizer beam but did not have the vertical glide slope beam.

The double standard of pilot experience for regularly scheduled commercial flights and for charter flights, and the inadequacy of the electronics system at Tri-State, apparently were the keys to the Huntington crash. Both could have been taken care of in advance by the FAA if it weren't for the shortsightedness of the agency's leadership.

This book is the story of some of that shortsightedness and how it hinders advancement in aviation safety. It details not only the incredibly poor management of the FAA, but the extraordinary lengths to which its leadership goes to cover up for its own deficiencies. It is also the story of my report, which evaluated the activities of a major part of the FAA; how it was received by the agency's leadership; how I was forced out of the FAA for daring to take this report to the top levels of FAA management, and how the government in general ignored the most important recommendations we had made—recommendations that could have saved hundreds of lives had they been put into effect.

CHAPTER II

ACTION THROUGH TRAGEDY

To understand the Federal Aviation Administration, an agency that employs fifty-eight thousand persons and spends $1.5 billion a year, it is necessary to know why and how it was created, what needs it is supposed to fill and what it is supposed to do.

It has been said that the FAA does not move forward on its own initiative—that whatever progress it has made has been in response to tragedy. In fact, the FAA itself was founded as the result of a tragedy—the in-flight collision over Grand Canyon on June 30, 1956, of a Trans World Airlines Super Constellation carrying seventy persons, and a United Air Lines DC-7 carrying fifty-eight passengers. The planes collided during a thunderstorm. There were no survivors. The planes had been flying in so-called uncontrolled airspace, which was not under the jurisdiction of the old Civil Aeronautics Administration. They were flying under rules that were essentially unchanged since the days of the old World War I "jennies" —in effect, "see and be seen."

The collision, of course, was just a symptom of the increasingly crowded conditions in the air above the United States. More and more travelers were taking to the air, as businessmen began to desert the railroads; the advent of newer, faster jet planes during the late 1950's hastened the switch. The production of light planes grew, too, doubling in the years from 1949 to 1958. New and improved models began to appear in larger numbers, and the number of private pilots doubled in the ten years that followed the end of World War II. Added to the growing civilian aircraft fleet were newer and faster military aircraft.

The military planes were not subject to control by normal civilian aviation authorities. In fact, control of civil aviation itself was fractionized—between the old Civil Aeronautics Administration, which had the task of operating the airways, and the Civil Aeronautics Board, which held authority over economic, regulatory and rule-making matters, including safety rules.

By 1957, domestic airlines were already flying about 3.6 million hours—or 13 percent of the total of all domestic flights. General aviation—private and corporate aircraft—were flying about 10.5 million hours, or 41 percent of the total. The military establishment was flying 12.1 million hours—or 46 percent of the total (nearly half of all domestic flights). In addition, there were two entirely separate systems of air traffic control: military and civilian.

As a result of this incredible growth and complexity of control, President Dwight D. Eisenhower in 1957 directed Edward P. Curtis, a former special assistant for aviation facilities and planning, to come up with some recommendations for the improvement of aviation development. Among the recommendations Curtis made was one to establish an independent federal aviation agency that would consolidate all of the essential management functions necessary to meet the common needs of military and civil aviation of the United States and prevent their plans from conflicting, as they had in the past. In the 1950's, for example, the Navy Department planned to install an airfield at New Iberia, Louisiana. There was, at the time, a municipal airport at Lafayette, Louisiana, which was used by general aviation and the airlines. Instrument landing system approaches to the Lafayette airport were to be from the north to the south. The Navy, meanwhile, planned, purchased the land for, and started laying concrete for the main runway of its training base at New Iberia, just eleven miles south of the Lafayette airport. An immediate conflict was obvious.

The answer, of course, was to give a single agency authority over all aviation safety matters. And as a result, in 1957, the Eisenhower administration proposed the creation of the FAA. Congress already had created the Airways Modernization Board, whose job it was to develop a common system for the management of air traffic —both civil and military. The final step was creation of a single agency that would regulate not only the system of airways, including the nationwide system of electronic aids to navigation, but safety in general, and specifically the certification of airmen and aircraft. It would also investigate aviation disasters.

Such was the Federal Aviation Agency. The plan for it

was placed before Congress in June of 1958 by General
Elwood R. (Pete) Quesada, chairman of the Airways
Modernization Board. Quesada had moved into that post
with impressive credentials. He had enlisted in the Army
in 1924 and had immediately taken flight training. By
1958 he had been an aviator thirty-four years and, as he
told the Senate Interstate and Foreign Commerce Committee's aviation subcommittee, "I stopped counting my
flying hours at about ten thousand, I suppose." During
World War II, Quesada had been in charge of setting
up the program of air navigational aids and systems that
made it possible to crowd the operations of thousands of
bombers into the limited airspace of the English Midlands,
keeping them flying under virtually impossible weather
conditions.

Quesada, who eventually became the first administrator
of the FAA and went on to become president and chairman of a major real-estate project in Washington, D.C.,
and a director of American Airlines, told the senators
why the administration wanted to create the FAA:

"Recent midair collisions, with tragic loss of human
life, have emphasized the need for action now to ac-
celerate corrective measures on two fronts:

"First, the development and application of improved
procedures and devices which will accomplish greater
effectiveness in the management of air traffic.

"Second, the establishment of a single Federal Aviation Agency into which are consolidated all the essential
management functions necessary to support the common
needs of military and civilian aviation."

Quesada argued that the new agency must be given
real authority over allocation and use of airspace by

both civil and military aircraft. Military participation was crucial to the successful consolidation of the essential management functions and required participation by military personnel in the activities of the new agency. Although this would be a civilian agency, national defense interests and military necessity would be recognized in controlling airspace.

A single authority for developing safety regulations, Quesada continued, must be designated in order to eliminate the duplication and confusion now caused by division of this responsibility among the Civil Aeronautics Board, the Civil Aeronautics Administration and the military establishment.

Rule-making was a technical problem requiring technical skills plus a background of operating experience. The single set of rules and the single national operation would lend itself to easy conversion in the event of a military emergency. Therefore, the legislation would assure a reserve bank of trained civilian personnel.

Quesada went on to explain that "one of the most serious problems confronting aviation is the increasing need for airspace by civil and military users. Present diffused responsibility for allotting airspace has contributed to a congested condition in large sectors of the country forcing serious inflexibilities upon both civil and defense operations. The committee method of assigning airspace on a case-by-case basis results in long debate, serious delay and patchwork solutions."

The proposed legislation won widespread approval from virtually all aviation interests. Stuart G. Tipton, president of the Air Transport Association—which represents the scheduled airlines—noted that "the American airspace has rapidly become a vanishing natural resource insofar as free access and capacity for safe operation of aircraft is concerned. The seemingly 'limitless ocean of air' has become quickly overcrowded." He strongly endorsed the legislation.

With the strong backing of the administration and the aviation community, Congress in 1958 authorized creation of the FAA. The new agency assumed the safety functions of all the existing regulatory boards, the first of which had been authorized as early as 1926, twenty-three years after the Wright brothers flew their first plane at Kitty Hawk, North Carolina.

The FAA actually came into being December 31, 1958. Its first task was to divide the airspace—safely and fairly —between military and civilian users. The immediate effect of this equitable division was to take sizable areas of formerly restricted military airspace and restore it to civilian use. Second, the FAA was to apply newly developed technical knowledge to modernize the airways. This entailed accelerated purchase and installation of electronic equipment, developing new traffic control procedures and training more air controllers.

To date the FAA has achieved only minimal success in modernizing the airways. This is an area in which the agency has failed miserably in its job of protecting the public.

CHAPTER III

THE OLD GUARD

My first contact with the FAA was during the first few weeks of its existence. I had known General Quesada during the seven years I spent as a budget officer in the office of the comptroller of the Secretary of Defense. Quesada was head of Air Force Reserve forces, and I was the budget reviewer for his organization. Many times during those years we sat across the table from each other as adversaries, and as a consequence we became well acquainted.

I left the Pentagon early in 1957 and moved to Van Nuys, California, where, at the invitation of my former boss at the Pentagon, Joseph Corie, who had become a vice president and comptroller of the Northrup Aviation Corporation, I accepted a post as director of financial controls at the firm's Van Nuys Division. After a couple of years there, I decided I wanted to return to Washington.

This was about the time the FAA was being created. I telephoned General Quesada one evening and he invited me to discuss the possibility of employment with Alan L. Dean, who was then an assistant administrator of the FAA. After a half-hour conference in Washington, Dean hired me. That was February 1959. I was brought aboard as a management analyst, Grade 15. (Civil Service jobs all have GS or "General Service" numbers. The highest is Grade 18, the lowest is Grade 1. The so-called "super grades" are GS 16, 17 and 18. These go to the level of agency management just below the ranking political appointees.)

Quesada in those early days was personally involved in pulling together the parts of several agencies into a single operating organization. His aim was to create an organization capable of controlling air traffic; administering safety; planning, financing and subsidizing airports; and designing, securing and installing the ground equipment systems such as communications and radar. These four jobs, of course, are what the FAA today is all about.

To organize his new agency, Quesada had three men to help: Dean, whom he had imported from the Bureau of the Budget (which, because of its reviewing functions over government spending and proposed legislation is actually one of the most powerful organizations in the executive branch of government); and Leonard Carulli and Howard Bull, both of whom had been in and out of government service several times. The very fact that Quesada imported people from outside the old CAA to organize the new agency was looked upon with considerable skepticism by the old guard—those who had sat behind desks at the CAA for twenty or thirty years (many of whom now occupy top jobs in the FAA).

In fact, shortly after the Federal Aviation Act was approved in 1958, and Quesada was appointed administrator, it was said that he refused to talk or even meet face to face with any CAA officials, including even top CAA Administrator James T. Pyle. Quesada simply didn't want them dominating the new agency—or even attempting to get a foot inside the door. He felt the way to do that was to keep the door closed. And he did—for months. Quesada believed that the CAA was loaded with incompetents occupying graded positions far higher than they deserved. He felt they lacked the proper educational background, and that their experience had been far too narrow. In short, he needed some bright younger people with fresh ideas. Had he relied on the old CAA people, they would have seen to it that no old practice was changed and that no new practice was instituted.

As a result, Quesada was able to make some moves that should have been made years earlier. For example, it had been common practice during aviation's earliest years for the pilot, during flight, to wander back through the plane greeting the passengers—probably calming the many for whom it was a first flight—and chatting with the little children aboard. The practice continued even though planes became far safer, and more and more passengers were frequent fliers who no longer needed their nerves calmed. Quesada recognized the danger in permitting the pilot frequent lengthy trips away from the cockpit, and he put an end to the practice. He told the pilots their job was in the cockpit, and they should stay there. Although it was a minor change, the pilots reacted fiercely because Quesada had violated this sacred practice of his predecessors. Eventually, though, the furor settled down, and the pilots put on their seat belts and remained in the cockpit.

He immediately changed another CAA policy. It had been the practice in CAA days that when an airplane showed some weakness—or developed a possibly serious engineering problem—the entire fleet of that model plane was grounded. Thus, a fleet of dozens to perhaps one hundred or two hundred aircraft might sit on the ground for weeks, while one suspicious airplane was examined, and every other plane of that same model was checked and inspected. Although that sounds conservative and in the interest of safety, it wasn't necessary.

Witness the old Lockheed Electra. The Electra had had some bad experiences—several had crashed. General Quesada personally investigated the problem and flew the airplane himself. He decided—and it was not a political decision or a snap judgment—that the problem did not warrant grounding the entire fleet. Instead, he slowed them down. Quesada consulted some expert aerodynamicists and concluded that at top speeds there was considerably greater risk of failure than at lower speeds. As a result, there was a speed limitation on the Electras for months —but he kept every plane in the air, aside from the few that were known to have real defects. And the airlines flew that fleet of planes, and used them for many months without mishap.

Quesada's decision had taken a great deal of courage. It would have been very easy to have grounded that entire fleet—and had he panicked or been unwilling to get the facts, to get expert help on the matter, that fleet likely would have been grounded. His move reflected too, what he thought of past CAA policy.

It was during those early days that I came to work for the FAA. (It was the Federal Aviation Agency in those days. It didn't become the Federal Aviation Administration until 1967 when it ceased to be a wholly independent agency and was transferred into the new Department of Transportation.) Quesada early discovered that the new organization was saddled with an exceedingly poor logistics organization—procurement, supply, inventory, warehousing and distribution. He decided that he was going to have a more efficient logistics organization, one which would be divided into two parts. He wanted both a policy organization and an operating organization. The policy side was something brand new —it was to set inventory standards, procurement policies and management practices which the other arm of the logistics department was to act on. Quesada and Dean asked me to take charge of this new procurement policy arm of the agency. That was about ten months after I arrived.

Such an organization, to be called the Materiel Policy Division, was to set standards so that, for example, we didn't have twenty years' worth of vacuum tubes at one warehouse and none in another warehouse. It meant that we set standards for procuring supplies not only through normal government purchasing channels, but for obtaining equipment through local suppliers across the nation so we could avoid having to store large quantities of materials at a large investment.

Certainly I had problems during those early months. Not the least of them was with many of the old CAA employees. They looked upon all of us newcomers with considerable distrust. They were afraid of us—because the new people came to the FAA at very high grades, higher than many employees who had been there for thirty years. We were a threat to them. And this manifested itself in a cynical, defensive posture that they adopted toward us.

I went into the new procurement job about February 1960, after spending the first ten to twelve months helping to put the right offices into the right squares on the organization chart. It wasn't long after I began my work of organizing the new logistics operation that I found we needed outside advice to lay out properly the kind of organization that Quesada wanted. I felt, for one thing, that a new logistics organization would be ineffective with the then present alignment of our engineering organization, because as things stood, the engineers tried to dominate the operation.

The FAA, I was beginning to find, was, as a House committee later concluded, an organization with more independent empires than medieval Europe.

CHAPTER IV

THE SUPPLY SCANDAL

No story of the Federal Aviation Administration could be complete without examining the supply and procurement system—a system whose operation is one of the biggest unpublicized scandals in government.

There is no way to measure how many needless deaths have occurred because FAA equipment either was not functioning properly—due to lack of spare parts—or because the most modern electronic equipment was not available to flight controllers, another result of inefficient supply operations.

The sloppiness with which the FAA permits its supply system to be run, while largely unknown to the public, is well known by those on the inside. It isn't as though the responsible FAA officials haven't been warned about their poor supply system—there has been an almost steady stream of fully documented reports highly critical of FAA supply operations since I joined the agency.

But time after time these reports were either ignored

by those in charge, or simply pushed aside, presumably because their publication or implementation might harm some member of the FAA "fraternity"—that cozy collection of middle and upper-middle management bureaucrats.

To understand the FAA supply system, you have to understand what it buys and where it stands in the overall FAA bureaucracy. The FAA is directed by a single administrator who is backed up by a deputy administrator. The FAA's headquarters organization, located in Washington, works under the administrator and his deputy in setting the policies and standards for everything the FAA does. There are, of course, the usual administrative, service and support functions in the agency, but the primary structure of the FAA with which this book deals consists of four parts.

First is the Air Traffic Service, which deals with the nation's aviation traffic. Second is the Airports Service, which deals with planning of airports and financial grants for them. Third is the engineering organization—essentially that run by an associate administrator for engineering and development. It includes systems research and development, a national experimental center, and related services. Its business is to carry out research and development, and to plan, service, and install the ground equipment used in navigation and control of air traffic. This equipment includes airport and long-range radar, instrument landing systems and a variety of communications equipment. The fourth major part of the agency is that which deals with safety, known in the FAA as the Flight Standards Service. It sets the policies and standards for the FAA's field organization to follow with respect to all safety matters concerned with civil aviation.

Of course, in addition to these main organizations, there are the usual finance, legal, medical and other support offices. During my last years at the FAA I was attached to the Office of Appraisal. In the military this would be known as the inspector general's office, and in private industry an office of internal audit. Its job—and I was the second-ranking official there—was to evaluate how well everything in the agency was going, and to keep the administrator apprised. We were also to make recommendations for improvements. (Ironically, although there was only one individual between the FAA administrator, John Shaffer—to whom we reported directly—and myself, as long as I worked in this office I never met him.)

Outside the Washington headquarters, the FAA is divided into ten regions, each of which includes several states. It is largely through regional offices that the public deals with the FAA. The operating activities of the FAA revolve about an investment by the taxpayers of nearly $2 billion. This includes the cost of airport control towers (although the federal government owns only two civil airports, it owns all the control towers) and their associated equipment, long-range navigational systems, airport instrument landing systems, radar and communications systems (and these often include expensive structures to house this equipment as well as the roads leading to otherwise inaccessible locations). To maintain existing systems and build new ones the FAA spends about $250 million a year buying everything from paper clips to multimillion-dollar radar installations, replacement parts and materials—as well as maintenance parts and services for the FAA's own fleet of more than one hundred aircraft.

For three years—from 1966 to 1969—I directed a staff that evaluated the FAA supply and procurement operation. We evaluated how production was going on at a variety of companies producing equipment for the FAA, and how the installation of this equipment was being accomplished throughout the nation by our government staff of installation people. We investigated the entire supply, spare parts, distribution and inventory levels of the agency. We also evaluated the negotiating, pricing and awarding of contracts for virtually everything that the agency bought.

All of these reports were addressed to Donald S. King, director of our section—the Installation and Materiel Service. But very little occurred. In fact, so little occurred that we had a saying in our small group that mimicked our director, Richard Leng, who used to write across the front page of our reports: "This should help." We never knew how, when, where or who these were helping, but we would always get that nice little glad hand in the form of his long-hand note: "This should help." The reason we never knew how these reports were helping is that Leng never implemented any of the recommendations in these reports at all.

Instead of fanning out the reports to the organizations which had been evaluated, he would send them back to us; and sometimes perhaps he would informally discuss their contents with the part of the FAA that had been evaluated.

The result, of course, is that between $4 million and

$7 million of the taxpayers' money—our salaries and expenses for those three years—wound up being wasted on valuable reports which went unheeded and were instead stuffed into file cabinets somewhere within the FAA. The real story of FAA supply policies is that millions of dollars' worth of advanced radar equipment lay wasted in warehouses instead of being installed in the air facilities where it was desperately needed to help provide safe air transportation. In at least one case—an examination of the FAA's Eastern Region—an undetermined amount of supplies, never posted to accounting records, was found lying about in warehouses, for the most part still in the original shipping crates. Furthermore, for manufacturing and installation jobs that producers said could be accomplished in six to eight months, it required up to five years for the FAA to complete budgetary, equipment procurement and installation phases.

These problems—which are commonplace within the agency—are not always hidden within the layers of the FAA's burdensome bureaucracy. There have been times when even the administrators knew about them—and in fact discussed them with the employees. One such administrator was Najeeb E. Halaby, who, after his departure from the FAA, served as chairman and chief executive officer of Pan American World Airways. Halaby was FAA administrator from 1961 to 1965.

In early 1962, when the FAA was experiencing considerable complaints from private industry about the agency's contracting practices, Halaby ordered me to arrange a procurement conference for a select group of FAA top management and supply personnel. Forty-one persons attended, including myself.

At the time, virtually every segment of the FAA had its own procurement department. Halaby, armed with studies by Harbridge House, a Cambridge, Massachusetts, research firm, urged the need for "one procurement organization working under common policies and ground rules rather than a procurement organization for each little empire that one would like to build." He then cited a few examples of the sloppiness of FAA procurement procedures that had resulted from the fractionalized purchasing policies of the old Civil Aeronautics Administration: "There is a case where, in one region, a contractor reported his profit was in the salvage value of a government building he was to demolish as part of a construction job. The government demolished the building and issued a change order and took the building away from the contractor. Now that doesn't indicate very good judgment to me.

"Another party learned, for the first time, that his property had been condemned (and used for a government facility) only when the tax collector returned his check for payment of his real-estate tax. Now that isn't public service at its best either."

In fact, it wasn't a "he," but a "she" who was involved; it was Representative Edward P. Boland, a Massachusetts Democrat, who called to the FAA's attention the problem of Mrs. Florence A. Deane of Springfield, Massachusetts. In a letter to the FAA's congressional liaison officer, Douglas Copley, on February 28, 1962, Boland wrote that Mrs. Deane was the owner, by inheritance from her mother, of real estate in Egg Harbor Township, New Jersey.

"Mrs. Deane has been paying taxes on this property

for many years," Congressman Boland wrote, "and this past November she sent her check to the tax collector of Egg Harbor Township. The check was returned with the note, 'I am returning your check as this property was taken over by the United States Government.' Mrs. Deane never received a notice of any taking by the government."

And that was how Mrs. Deane discovered the FAA had acquired her property—without telling her—for use in its National Aviation Facilities Experimental Center near Atlantic City, New Jersey.

Halaby tried his hardest to break away from the old CAA way of doing things, and plugged for his proposed unified supply system: "I am told both within and without the agency that the age-old problem of engineers, inspectors, contracting officers, all being the agency spokesman, telling the contractor what to do and how to do it, is a continuing problem here, too. Now I don't know how anyone solves this, but by being decisive and disciplined, in having one spokesman for the agency in anything affecting the contractual administration. And it is certainly my policy; in fact, I don't know of any alternative to having one man responsible for the financial and legal commitments involved in any procurement contract. I am not saying that it should always be one or the other type of man, but I am just saying there must be *one*, and he must speak for *one* agency."

Long before Halaby's talk, however, we had discovered how inefficient the FAA supply operation was. The FAA's supply systems hadn't been examined since the 1953–1955 period when it was still the CAA. Although it was supposed to have been reorganized when the CAA was transformed into the FAA in 1958, the supply and procurement arm still hadn't been changed or examined, despite the fact that the agency's annual spending had increased from $23 million in 1954 to $224 million by 1961 when the FAA was supposedly trying to upgrade the nation's air traffic control system on a priority basis.

During the fifteen months from December 1959 through mid-March 1961 a number of preliminary examinations of FAA's supply and procurement operations were made. Some of the results were that a series of audits by the General Accounting Office and the FAA's own internal auditing group disclosed what were then considered "many unbusinesslike practices which have tended to incur unnecessary costs or risks." Spot checks of inventories reflected many instances of large excess stock. In one instance, excess vacuum tubes worth more than $2.5 million were uncovered.

Many instances of unsound procurement practices were also disclosed. For example, in the Bureau of Research and Development a large majority of procurement was being negotiated with single companies "by interested technical personnel. Audit reports also revealed that insufficient effort was made by procurement personnel in that bureau to establish the capability of proposed contractors to accomplish the work contemplated. In many instances, contractor-estimated costs were not adequately reviewed in the negotiation process." In several instances, contractors were permitted to overrun contract costs without proper review by FAA procurement offices. Often too procurement personnel had forfeited their responsibility to engineering personnel who were untrained in supply operations.

One of the most serious problems was the fact that

"when in some instances poor practices have been brought to the attention of procurement and inventory management personnel, an almost defiant or 'so what' attitude has been demonstrated."

Many of these problems never were cleared up. This became evident through continuing reports by our own evaluation group in later years, reports that went nowhere but into metal filing cabinets. Not only did our reports document specific instances of mismanagement and just plain sloppiness, but, as in the examinations in the FAA's early years, nobody seemed very interested in clearing them up. Knowing the FAA—and the attitude of the CAA personnel, many of whom still are at work in the FAA—most of the inefficiencies we found probably still exist today.

The results of this sloppiness make themselves felt as part of the cost of running the FAA, which is borne by the taxpayers who obviously are paying far more than they should because of this huge amount of inefficiency. In fact, we were able to illustrate just how inefficient the FAA supply system was when, during the spring of 1961, we examined it in comparison with the Western Electric Co. We chose Western Electric, which supplies and distributes equipment to the American Telephone & Telegraph Company's Bell System, because its operations were found to closely parallel those of FAA.

What we found was that while Western Electric was processing any requisition in a single day, we were averaging ten days for a regular procurement request, seven days when we were in a special hurry, and reached one-day processing only when we needed the supplies in an emergency. It was only in 0.6 percent of procurement cases that Western Electric failed to have the required supplies on hand, while FAA's supply organization was out of stock 7 percent of the time. Also, while it cost $4.76 at Western Electric for every $100 worth of supplies ordered, that cost being borne by Bell System companies and, ultimately, the telephone user, at FAA, where the taxpayer foots the bill, it cost $17.95 to order every $100 worth of supplies.

What contributed greatly to these conditions was the manner in which the FAA was organized with its widely splintered operating authority within the agency. This system, we said, encouraged widely varied practices within the agency and precluded establishing in one point agency-wide responsibility for sound, businesslike practices.

As the supply system was set up, it was virtually impossible for the administrator to pin down who was *really* responsible for what, and who was accountable for the results—either good or bad. This, of course, was precisely what the old-guard long-time Civil Aeronautics Administration management wanted: muddy the waters and then nobody knows who to blame for anything. Our recommendation was that operation of all supply functions throughout the FAA be assigned to one division. We suggested that the division be located directly under the assistant administrator for management services, who would be responsible directly to the administrator. This would provide the agency, we believed, with one focal point for sound management and operation of all supply functions.

To study the problem and its solutions, I recommended that Halaby retain an outside consulting firm. Harbridge

House of Cambridge, Massachusetts, was hired in early 1961 to undertake the project. The idea for retaining Harbridge House—or any other outside firm, for that matter —was not unanimously supported within the FAA. One reason for this, of course, was that I had suggested it. And after all, I'd been in the FAA only two years; what right did I—a virtual outsider—have to come in and recommend overhauling something that had been in effect for decades.

In fact, the assistant administrator for management services, Alan L. Dean, wrote a brief note to Administrator Halaby about the plans for the Harbridge House report. He noted that representatives of the Bureau of Facilities and Materiel, the Bureau of Research and Development, and the Office of General Counsel had participated in drawing up an outline of the matters Harbridge House would examine. "They have concurred," Dean wrote, "with the exception that Mr. Tippets has expressed reservations concerning the advisability of having Harbridge House make recommendations on the proper organization of the materiel function." Joseph H. Tippets was then head of the Bureau of Facilities and Materiel, which was responsible for supply and procurement. Harbridge House eventually recommended abolition of that bureau and, with a bureaucrat's instinct for survival, he had objected.

By September of 1961 the Harbridge House report was completed. It was a stinger, a revolutionary document to the old fraternity. There were a lot of organizational changes; an awful lot of people, especially in engineering, got scrambled as a result of what Harbridge House proposed, which Halaby approved. And oddly enough, it wasn't really Harbridge House that got the blame from the old bureaucrats. It was Phil Ryther, that new man who'd led Harbridge House to change the old order of things. And if I hadn't gotten some idea of how my original recommendation to hire Harbridge House would drastically affect my own future, the almost immediate repercussions of the report soon changed that. Barely had Halaby accepted Harbridge House's report and begun placing the recommendations into effect, when I found myself practically out of a job.

CHAPTER V

BANISHED TO THE LIBRARY

Harbridge House recommended, among other things, taking my office—the Materiel Policy Division—out from under the direct control of the assistant administrator (Alan Dean) and transferring it over to the engineering organization where it was to be made part of the new Installation and Materiel Service.

I had become known as the bad guy, of course, in connection with the Harbridge House matter because of my role in retaining the firm and in spearheading its study. And now I found myself subordinate to those who opposed the study, primarily the old CAA fraternity.

There were those—including myself—who thought that I would be the logical individual to direct the procurement organization of the entire FAA, directly subordinate to the director of the Installation and Materiel Service. However, I was not selected for that job. As a matter of fact, I wasn't really selected for any job in the new organization. Since no move was made to abolish my old organ-

ization—or at least my job as head of it—I remained for
some time as chief of the Materiel Policy Division. Ad-
mittedly, we weren't always busy, but we did manage to
accomplish some things. One was to spearhead another
examination—called Project Pipeline—of the supply and
procurement activities of the FAA.

The idea for Project Pipeline was mine, although the
name was not. The name like the agency itself, as we have
seen, represented a combination of the military and the
civilian. One thing that came over with the military side
was the way in which it named things—Project Pipeline,
Project Searchlight, Project Beacon. Like the military,
too, there were the acronyms. The FAA has always been
a great place for acronyms, so much so that to the casual
observer the agency appears to have a language all its
own, comprising largely sets of frequently unpronounce-
able initials, the meanings of which completely escape
the outsider. So prolific had the use of acronyms become
that by 1970 even Congress was having a difficult time
translating them. Here's an example of some of FAA jargon:

"After DPC was cancelled out in 1961, SRDA began
work on a system design for NAS Stage A. Subsequently,
IBM was given a contract for the initial CCC for installation at JAX with systems development to be performed
both there and at NAFEC. With SPO in charge of the
program, Raytheon was given a contract for the CDC
and, subsequently, when work on the development of
this unit fell behind schedule, the work on the permanent
CCC was fragmented into NAS Stage A Mod. 1-a and b,
NAS Stage A Mod. 2, Versions 1 and 2, and NAS Stage
A Mod. 3d. Proceeding under IOC implementation of

FDP, IBM designed a temporary system for some of the high volume ARTC's with the intention of replacing these temporary systems with the permanent Stage A Mod. 1 Version 2, with CUE capability. Meanwhile, RD 100 and RD 200 in R&D were involved in development of TRACON capability to augment the ASR's, RAPCON's and RATCC's. Subsequently, it was decided to go with ARTs III, II, I and Ia in lieu of TRACON, and a contract was let to UNIVAC for the development of this equipment."

After reprinting that paragraph in a report on the FAA, a House committee urged the agency to henceforth restrict its use of acronyms.

Project Pipeline was a short way of saying that the FAA had decided to examine its whole purchasing organization from the point when a need is determined for a specific item, to the buying, warehousing, distributing, and the actual placing of it into the hands of the individual who is finally going to hook it up to a piece of machinery and use it.

Representatives of all branches of FAA logistics took part in the project during mid-1961. Case Institute of Technology was hired as a consultant.

Project Pipeline's recommendations covered a wide variety of supply functions, including the conversion of scattered warehousing operations to a single, centralized warehouse to serve as an agency-wide supply center. The report—parts of which were bitterly contested by the old CAA clique—forecast that if its recommendations were placed into effect, the FAA would save more than $13.5 million at one shot, and an additional $4.5 million annually. Much of this would result from cutting back

on inventory. So concerned did those then in charge of
FAA procurement become over the Project Pipeline recommendations that in one case the acting director of the
Aviation Facilities Service, Donald S. King, urged that
the report be suppressed, especially outside the FAA.
"We are compelled," he wrote, "in the best interests of the
agency, to recommend that this portion of the report be
entirely disregarded and that it not be further circulated
under any circumstances, particularly outside the agency.
This recommendation is motivated by the conviction that
the Pipeline projection . . . is extravagant beyond possible realization even under the most ideal conditions." He
suggested that at best no more than a third of the savings
projected by Pipeline could be achieved. Judging from
his concern and language, Pipeline must have been dead
right.

In any case, partly because of the reorganization that
followed Pipeline, and partly because of my own reputation for not caring whose reputation is hurt in one of my
evaluation reports, I was given virtually nothing to do in
the months that followed. I had all the accouterments
that befitted my grade: a secretary, a plush wall-to-wall
carpet, a spot in the executive parking lot, the ubiquitous
chrome water bottle (amply filled with ice water) found
on the desks of all government executives; the only thing
I didn't have was something to do.

As a result, in mid-1962 I approached my boss, Donald
S. King, who was director of the Installation and Materiel
Service and a long-time CAA bureaucrat. I approached
him because the Materiel Policy Division, of which I was
chief, had finally been transferred from the Office of Man-

agement Services to Installation and Materiel as Harbridge House had recommended.

I explained to King that I hoped my industrial as well as government experience would be of value in this new venture, and that I wanted him to know that "I'm very interested in being part of the management of the program."

King looked at me stonily. "I'm making no commitments to anybody, Phil, but I'll keep your remarks in mind."

The brief interview was over.

The days dragged by and I began to feel (and this was reinforced later by friends) that I was being kept in limbo because I had spearheaded at least two projects which were highly controversial within the FAA: Harbridge House and Pipeline. I had committed the cardinal sin: I had been too zealous in my work. I was to find out years later that any extra zeal is not appreciated in the FAA.

About the middle of June 1962, as the details of the new supply organization became clearer, I discussed again my lack of work with King.

"Phil, I've been over your record and frankly I'm very impressed with it," King told me. "I might say that from the standpoint of experience and performance you're equal with—or perhaps ahead of—anyone else being considered for one of the openings we've got."

I discussed my lack of work also with Robert Shank, an associate administrator and King's superior, who was head of engineering and other organizations. He, too, appeared impressed with my background, both in and out of government.

Then, on August 3, 1962, King called me into his office, saying he wanted to discuss working arrangements between the procurement operation and the general counsel's office. But this matter had barely been touched upon when suddenly he opened the question of my assignment.

"You are one of the most intelligent people I've ever met, Phil," he said. "In fact, you appear to me to be completely honest, and forthright, and you manage to get things done. But you've got one fault—you're a stormy person. And frankly I've got to tell you that based on this I cannot appoint you chief of our procurement division— nor, in fact, assistant chief. But I'll do my best to put you on the staff and help you retain your GS 16. How does that sound?"

I was totally surprised. I didn't really know what to say, and I told him just that. Apparently, he mistook my surprise for desperation.

"Just how desperate are you?" he asked. I assured him that I had excellent personal control and he should have no fear that I was to any extent desperate. I asked him then where he had gotten the idea I was a "stormy person." Had he discussed this with my bosses over the past fifteen years? He had not—but he indicated he had checked indirectly with the Northrup Corporation, and had received an excellent reference from the comptroller, for whom I had worked.

Had he checked with Lyle Garlock, an assistant secretary of the Air Force for whom I'd worked for many years? No, he had not.

Had he even checked with Alan Dean in his own agency, the FAA? He had—and Dean had given me the highest recommendation.

Had this information come from FAA people? King said it had not.

"Well, then, Don, what's the basis for saying I'm a stormy person?"

"Phil, let's just say it comes from someone outside of the FAA."

Then King really opened up. "Phil, some of your activities around here have severely embarrassed me, and made me feel like a fool. For instance, isn't it true that you informed the administrator [Najeeb Halaby] about the difficulty we had with the condemnation of land at Dulles Airport?"

I told him I had not.

"Well, I was sorely embarrassed by Halaby's reference to this at the procurement conference last April."

I told King that I thought he was wrong since this matter was not brought up at the conference some four months ago, and that the only land condemnation problem mentioned dealt with a Massachusetts woman who had owned some land near Atlantic City, New Jersey, which was brought to Halaby's attention by a congressman.

Then King asked whether I had informed Halaby about the case in San Diego in which a contractor was to salvage a government building as part of his fee on an installation contract. The FAA itself, however, had dismantled the building and put through a contract change to cover its actions. The contractor had come to Washington to discuss the matter with agency lawyers. Halaby had mentioned that incident in his April talk.

"To be honest, Phil, I think you had Halaby bring these matters up at the procurement conference just to embarrass me. And furthermore, I've always had a suspicion that the only reason you brought in Harbridge House was simply to further your own ambitions."

"That's ridiculous. I had never formed a personal ambition in the Harbridge House study," I said, "although it is true that afterward I had hoped to head the materiel function."

"Well, I have a different understanding. I think you had ambitions much higher than that. Phil, I really don't know why I'm discussing this matter with you at all. As you know, I have the authority to make appointments around here, and the only mistake I can see that I've made is to tell you the reason why I'm doing it. And that's something I don't have to do, but I think I'm just trying to be fair to you in doing it."

After several more weeks of silence following the King meeting, I made another appointment to see Robert Shank. We met on September 28, 1962, and the conversation was very cordial. He promised to do something about getting me something to do.

It wasn't until November 23 that I heard from him again, at a meeting in his office that I had requested. He said he had hoped he could work out a suitable arrangement for a position for me in the Installation and Materiel Service, and that he had brought the matter to some of the directors in the service. He was told, he said, that their subordinates would not "stand still" for such an arrangement, and since he didn't want to violate the management principle of assigning some one under incompatible conditions, he didn't feel he should proceed with the matter.

Finally, fed up with the whole business, I wrote a four-

page letter to Najeeb Halaby, the administrator. I reminded him that I had spearheaded the Harbridge House
study, Project Pipeline, the establishment of agency inventory policy and many procurement policies, the cata-
loging of agency inventories, the return to the supply depot of millions of dollars of excess inventories from the
field and the establishment of the spare parts provision-
ing policy of the agency. I ended by saying, "I am proud
of these things even though they seem to have characterized me as a 'stormy person.'"

The result of the letter was a long talk in Halaby's office on December 17, 1962. He wound up the conversation
by offering me the post of executive officer—third in
command—of the Installation and Materiel Service, subject to the concurrence of Richard Leng, who was to become director of the Installation and Materiel Service
early in 1963.

Leng and I discussed the appointment a few days after he arrived and, sensibly, he said he wanted a few
weeks to examine his new domain before agreeing. Several weeks later, in early March, he called me and told me
that those with whom I would work—namely the old CAA
gang—had almost unanimously come to him and told him
what a terrible thing I had done by bringing Harbridge
House in to study the agency. It just wouldn't work for
me to be brought into the upper levels of FAA management.

Again I complained to Halaby, this time in a letter of
March 6, 1963. Leng had not discussed his decision with
the administrator, but Leng and Robert Shank had
agreed that I should not be promoted. "Mr. Leng says I

have a reputation of being very competent," I wrote, "but too critical of the way others do things.

"I grant that perhaps Dale Carnegie's technique may have it all over mine, but the fact of the matter is that many of the things that are haunting me, because they ruffled some feathers, are things which you directed be done over the strong objections of the old Aviation Facilities Service—'Pipeline'—'Harbridge House'—the procurement conference last spring.

"This situation has been going on almost a year. It's been real tough on me and I'm anxious to pursue some other courses. I have two or three ideas I would like to discuss with you."

The matter rested for a while. Then, on April 29, nearly a month and a half after the letter to Halaby, I received a letter that my post, that of chief of the Materiel Policy Division, was being abolished. The same letter offered me the post of deputy assistant administrator for appraisal—the second-ranking job in the Office of Appraisal, in effect, the FAA administrator's inspector general's office.

I immediately accepted the appointment. But my happiness was short-lived. A month later—on May 24—I was told that the position of deputy assistant administrator in the Office of Assistant Administrator for Appraisal itself was being abolished. Therefore, I was told to remain in my present position "until such time as an appropriate position can be located. At that time, you will be issued another reduction-in-force notice." (This second letter had been handed to me by Richard Leng—and it apparently meant that the old guard didn't want me in a job as sensitive as that of appraising the quality of their work and reporting directly to the administrator. I was being told, in effect, that somebody was looking for someplace to put me.)

At the same time that Leng handed me the letter advising me that the appraisal job had fallen through, he handed me a memorandum concerning a job he wanted me to undertake. Leng's memo recalled that "from time-to-time certain statements have been made with regard to excessive costs in connection with the establishment of air navigation and air traffic control facilities."

The latest of these statements, he said, was to be the theme of a speech to be made by Siegburt B. Poritzky, then the manager of navigation for the Air Transport Association, the trade organization of the scheduled airlines. My job was to somehow prove that this was an ill-conceived and ill-considered complaint by ATA, as the FAA management thought a legitimate complaint was impossible.

I declined to take on the assignment at first, but said I would think about it for a day or so and come up with my own plan of action. I presented my plan the next day. It called for my being authorized to select any three persons from the FAA, and to retain three outside consultants from whatever source I wanted. My plan was accepted. Among those I selected were FAA employees from the Los Angeles, Kansas City and Washington offices. I also chose an associate professor from Case Institute in Cleveland, the president of an electronics firm near San Francisco, and the retired president of an electronics company in Seattle.

Although we were detailed to study all of the statements which had been made that were critical of the

FAA's electronics installations and policies, the best was probably Poritzky's which said, in effect, that the FAA was paying four to five times too much for what it was getting, and as a result couldn't install very much electronics equipment on the appropiations we were receiving.

For example, Poritzky examined the instrument landing systems (ILS) and found that in three years, since 1960, the FAA budget estimates had risen 42 percent for such devices. "The curious thing is that ILS did not change significantly in the intervening years. The over-all U.S. commodity price index has risen only 2.7 percent since 1960."

Then he gave a few specifics: "Let's consider something simple. The runway end identification light system (REIL). FAA budget cost is $18,200. An REIL, as you know, consists of two light fixtures in appropriate housings, with flashing lights inside. FAA budgets $18,200 for an REIL installation. The State of Minnesota budgets $3,000 for lights to serve exactly the same purpose."

For 75-megacycle fan marker: "FAA's estimate [was] $25,800. The State of Nebraska estimates about $3,250 for a dual marker, complete. A dual equipment commercial 75 megacycle marker is sold by Wilcox Electric as a package ready to install on two telephone poles for $2,413. Let's assume that instead of Nebraska's and Wilcox's $1,000 estimates for installation, we take twice the cost of the Wilcox package itself as the price to install and provide power and control to this marker—for a total of $7,230. FAA's estimates is still more than three times higher."

Poritzky found several reasons why FAA's costs were

so high: "An important one is that the method by which the federal government must purchase is infinitely more cumbersome than the manner in which you or I would buy and install radio equipment. The government uses elaborate means to protect itself against the unscrupulous bidder, and to protect itself against its own people. While you and I can arbitrarily use our previous experience and our judgment in picking the contractors we like, the government must go through procurement procedures which are eminently fair to all of the prospective bidders, but which run the costs up and which unfortunately still do not guarantee good performance."

But he found other reasons as well. He found that the government was dedicated to providing capabilities and design features in its equipment which were nice to have but "which are not essential to good performance."

Take the case of remote control radio stations. Not only were most of the costs associated with such facilities higher for the federal government (because engineering and freight were higher though the actual cost of equipment was lower), but the difference in the costs of construction and materials was incredible. The government figured it would cost more than $52,000 to build a remote control radio facility and its housing. Aeronautical Radio Inc., a system run by the airlines, figured the cost of construction and materials at less than $2,000. "Even if we assume that the FAA facilities are installed at difficult sites so that construction costs are high, we still end up with just a little building out in the boondocks," Poritzky said.

The difference, of course, was that the FAA was constructing these little buildings like fortresses, while the commercial airlines were achieving virtually the same equipment reliability in a cheaper building.

Poritzky analyzed some of the reasons that the government paid more. One was that states and airlines, which maintain their own navigational aids in many cases, buy equipment built to commercial standards, the manufacturer's aim being to make a well-performing facility "and not to meet a myriad of specifications on components, sub-assemblies and gold plating. . . . We must question the old assumption that the only equipment which can be good is equipment which specifically meets FAA's detailed product and component specifications. We have more than ample experience in commercial use of both ground and airborne equipment which proves that equipment built by reputable manufacturers to commercial standards, bought by knowledgeable buyers, has a performance record equal to or better than FAA equipment."

And Poritzky knew whereof he spoke. He had worked for the CAA. And what's more, we found that he was about 99 percent right.

Our report, confirming Poritzky's examination and the other criticisms from ATA, was sent to Halaby, who became so excited about it that he finally decided to put me to work. All of a sudden there was created a brand new organization in the director's office at the Installation and Materiel Service. It was to be known as the Evaluation Division, and I was named its chief. It was our job to examine just how well the Installation and Materiel Service was doing its job. However, working directly for Leng was not destined to be a bed of roses. It was during the next couple of years that Leng studiously ignored our many reports, placing on most of them his bright little handwritten note: "This should help."

But one study that he apparently didn't feel would help was one entitled Project Management—a report on evaluation of the Program Management Division in the Installation and Materiel Service. It was completed in March 1965. It was, as its title implies, designed to evaluate the management of the Program Management Division, the principal engineering organization in FAA, which was indeed poor.

For one thing, although the primary function of the division was engineering, only 56 of its 206 employees could even remotely be considered engineers. To better understand this situation, it must be explained that several years previous to this report a mass redevelopment plan was put into motion. There were three groups of employees: the first group comprised employees selected to remain because of their acceptable productivity; the second group was to be reassigned elsewhere because their functions had been transferred; the third group comprised employees who were encouraged to seek employment elsewhere, transfer or retire. The plan envisioned the remaining staff as a hard core to be expanded by bringing in new high-caliber engineers. But, as with many such plans in the FAA, this one had not been carried out to any appreciable degree. Of the 206 positions that were filled in this "engineering" organization, we found that 10 were on detail elsewhere in the FAA; 20 were considered nonproducers who were supposed to go elsewhere; 42 were in effect record-keepers; 60 were stenographers, typists and clerks, and 15 were program managers and administrative types. That left 56 engineering personnel as the backbone of the organization. Within the organization, 63 jobs were titled "engineer" for Civil Service record-keeping purposes. Of these, no engineering was being accomplished in 22 positions; less than 25 percent actual engineering was accomplished in another 14; and only in 27 of the jobs was any more than 25 percent of the time being occupied in engineering.

Bear in mind that this was 1965 and engineers were in wide demand. The FAA was nevertheless still not using its real engineering manpower with proper discretion. The nonengineering tasks such as materiel control, physical and fiscal project control, clerical and coordination duties were the ones being performed by the engineers.

Quality was another story still. We found that of 108 engineering jobs in the agency in the GS 12 through GS 17 grades, only 61 percent were held by graduate engineers and only 14 percent were registered professional engineers. "It may be significant that in an electronic engineering environment only three are registered professional engineers [electronic]," we wrote, adding, "This is not to say that a nongraduate or nonregistered engineer is not a good one, but such a low percentage of academic and professional recognition does invite inquiry."

We found also that there was a lack of purpose, drive or initiative that would otherwise have encouraged registration, for the electronics industry as a whole was achieving staggering new developments. As we noted: "Yet, we find that in an electronic engineering environment such as in the Program Management Division, there are only a few scattered individuals who have enough initiative to keep up with the most challenging state of the art.

"We find that in some areas, the study of periodicals and technical journals on government time has been discouraged. This lack of professional attitude is further reflected in the absence of any planned training of our currently employed personnel or a planned program for recruitment of current engineering college graduates. For the past three years there has been little or no recruitment of college graduates and such training of incumbent personnel has been on an isolated and on a 'need now' basis."

We found in general that employee morale was low, particularly in areas where although job descriptions were approved, those holding the jobs were acting at the lower pay grades at which they had been working before the reorganization. Other causes of low morale and inefficient operations found were difficulties in filling vacancies; obsolescence of some job descriptions; inequality of pay grades in areas where two individuals were performing identical functions; promotion restrictions; frustration due to inability of the Systems Research and Development Service to furnish specifications and drawings on schedule; and at best a hazy concept of program management itself.

The report had some distribution around the FAA and, as a result, Leng and the others involved in management of the Installation and Materiel Service were highly embarrassed by it. The result of Leng's unhappiness was not long in making itself known. On May 10, a Monday morning, I arrived in my office to find on my desk a brief memorandum from Leng dated the previous Friday: "You

are advised . . . that you are temporarily assigned to my
immediate office to perform special assignments under
my direct supervision and orders. The assignment will
require your absence from the evaluation staff, and I
will, therefore, designate a person to act in your absence."

In short, I had been relieved of my position, moved
out of my office and banished to a cubbyhole across from
the FAA library. I was being punished for doing my job,
for directing the preparation of a report that turned out
to reflect adversely on my boss.

And what was Leng's special assignment for me? When
I walked into Leng's office that Monday to discuss this
"special assignment," he handed me a sheet of lined
scratch paper on which he had scrawled the following
note:

"Assignment:

"Examine in the Library of Congress the evaluation
techniques used by industry (and other government
agencies if possible). I am particularly interested in the
size of the staff used by others, the method of reporting,
the level to which this staff reports, etc. Take a week's
look at this and report back Monday 5/17 to see if additional time is required."

After noticing that my leg was in a plaster cast (I had
been in an automobile accident some weeks earlier), Leng,
without a sound, scratched out another note:

"Due to your medical problems it is not wise for you to
go to the Library of Congress. Therefore, please conduct
this investigation in our 10th floor library.

"Simultaneously, I am relieving you of your supervisory

duties as chief, Evaluation Staff so that you can devote full time to this special assignment."

The next day I decided to discuss this new assignment with Leng. I suggested that if he wanted a really thorough job on the evaluation techniques used by government and industry I would have to contact other government agencies to find out just how they accomplished their evaluations. At the meeting, Leng specifically refused to allow me to talk with the Defense Department, private industry, universities or even any of the authorities on management.

Barely had I gotten into that assignment when Leng sent me another missive: I was to be reassigned again, this time to Cletus Estep, the chief of the Materiel Management Division, who would give me "a series of assignments which will be directed toward literature search type of activities." Then Leng added an interesting admonition: he forbade me to look into any files of either the Program Management Division or the Procurement Division—presumably a move to keep me from further embarrassing him.

Meanwhile, I had complained about this harassment to Lieutenant General Harold W. Grant, the deputy administrator. Appended to my complaint was a copy of the evaluation staff report on the Project Management Division. Whether it was through General Grant's intervention or not I do not know, but within three or four months my temporary assignment ended and I was back at work evaluating.

But it wasn't my last encounter with Leng. On November 6, 1964, I was called into Leng's office to discuss an increase in salary which I had been due to receive on September 27 of that year. Leng showed me two copies of a form he was to fill out in connection with the increase, a form of periodic salary increase that is virtually automatic as long as an employee is performing satisfactorily. The papers he showed me are entitled "Certification of Level of Competence for Within-Grade Increases." Such forms are routinely filled out by supervisors in connection with these pay raises.

Leng had signed and completed both forms which he showed to me. One was dated the previous day, and on it he had indicated that I was not working at an acceptable level of competence. (In fact, in the remarks section which he showed to me, he had written: "This confirms my discussion with you of a few weeks ago in which I expressed considerable satisfaction & pride in your general accomplishments. *However, at the same time I told you that I was still unhappy with your violent explosions.* This hurts you, the I&M Service & FAA. Your other contributions are of such magnitude that I intend to re-review this on 12/6 and am confident I will be able to certify your within-grade increase at that time.")

The second form was signed and dated December 6, 1964, a month hence, and on it he indicated I was working at an acceptable level of competence. He said he intended to file both of them with the personnel office. At the time, it seemed strange to me that, while my performance was not acceptable as of yesterday, it was possible to look thirty days into the future and know that my performance would be acceptable by then.

By the following February, however, I still had not heard anything about my raise and of course had not seen the money. I drafted a letter to the administrator in which I mentioned having recently "observed a piece of administration in the agency concerning a relatively minor matter but which was handled in a manner that none of us can be very proud of. I also feel that as a senior member of the agency evaluations staff it is my duty to not turn my head from such a thing."

I proceeded to detail the entire matter. But I never sent the letter. I showed it to Clement E. Mayhall, who was second in command in the Logistics Service. He told his boss, Donald S. King, who, as deputy director of the Logistics Service, was Leng's deputy.

King phoned me at home that evening and urged me not to send it. The same evening, Nelson Jump, the FAA's personnel officer, telephoned me at nine o'clock to advise that official action had been taken—no doubt coincidentally—that day, February 23, 1965, and that my raise would be retroactive to the preceding September.

I had finally received my pay raise, five months late.

Leng left shortly afterwards and was replaced by Don King, a man whose chief aim in life appeared to be keeping everybody happy.

CHAPTER VI

KEEPING THEM HAPPY

During the midautumn of 1966, a five-member evaluation
team under my direction examined the Procurement
Operations Division, the section of the FAA responsible
for the agency's multimillion-dollar purchasing program.
Tho division had been reorganized earlier in 1966, and
this was a follow-up inspection to one done earlier in the
year.

The team found, among other things, that because of a
prolonged delay in effecting the reorganization there were
serious personnel problems. There was an atmosphere of
instability in day-to-day operations, as a result of which
procurement functions were either not being accomplished at all or frequently were not being accomplished
properly.

Many of the problems we found reflected seriously on
the management of the division. The prolonged delay in
completing the reorganization, for example, had created
an atmosphere of uncertainty which virtually ruined employee morale. Employees complained of insecurity. In all,

the reorganization supervisors were changing too frequently and there were simply too many bosses. Furthermore, the bosses lacked leadership, and too little assistance and guidance was coming from supervisors. There was no on-the-job training, nor any encouragement to update skills and knowledge, which led to a general lack of direction in the work being done. The supervisors were disinterested in ideas or suggestions coming from employees. There was favoritism, and management seldom let the employees know of upcoming changes that would affect them. Management was simply not interested in the employees.

Much of the staff morale problem was uncovered through discussions with the employees. The report noted that "whether these assertions are true or untrue, the sheer magnitude of complaints should be a significant concern to management and not be dismissed as 'simply the gripes of disgruntled employees.'"

As could be easily predicted, these morale problems translated themselves into serious problems which resulted in the taxpayer getting another raw deal from the FAA. In the area of documentation of purchases, for example, highly significant backup papers for purchases were missing from the files. Evidence of legal clearance of findings and determinations was missing from a number of files. Under FAA purchasing procedures, the agency is required to make a "finding and determination" that a specific piece of equipment should be bought, how much should be purchased and from which firm it should be obtained. All of these are to be approved by the FAA's legal department before the purchase is made. Evidence that the lawyers had examined these justifications was missing and as a result much of the material had been improperly acquired.

Another FAA form, used to determine whether a proposed contractor is responsible—whether the contractor has the financial strength to complete the contract, whether he can do the job in a technically correct manner, whether his quality control procedures are sufficient to meet the FAA's exacting requirements, whether he has adequate management to get the job done—was not in the files at all. As a result, we had to assume that the procurement department was not making these determinations, and as a result contracts may possibly have gone to companies with inadequate quality control. (What if poor quality control had passed a radar device that later broke down during operations at a busy metropolitan airport?)

Missing from the files also were copies of another FAA form, on which procurement officers are supposed to list a summary of what each corporation bidding for a job proposes to provide: prices, delivery dates and the like. These forms are supposed to be completed to make certain various bids can be easily compared and that the government gets the best possible deal.

Similarly missing was a so-called synopsis of proposed procurements. This synopsis is published and widely circulated to hundreds of companies across the nation. It provides them with a list of items the FAA is planning to purchase and gives them a chance to bid on the projects. If these listings are not circulated—and evidence was lacking that they had been circulated—then certainly many companies had no way of knowing what the FAA intended to buy, and therefore couldn't bid on the jobs, so that the government may well have lost out on the best product at the lowest possible price.

Absent also from the documentation files were the completed forms that contained the contractors' representations and certifications for negotiated contracts. When the government negotiates with a firm, as opposed to publicly advertising for bids, the firm is supposed to make certain certifications concerning prices, costs and profits. And an official of the company must certify that these are honest costs for parts, labor and the like. In many cases the files showed that the FAA was not getting this information. This, of course, meant that when a company said it wanted to charge a certain amount and didn't include a breakdown of the cost of major parts, we really had no basis for knowing whether or not these prices were legitimate.

These problems with documentation were for major purchases; we found, though, that even small purchases were being handled sloppily. For example, in many cases purchase orders were being sent to contractors still in the original FAA engineer's jargon. The result was in some cases that the contractor didn't know what he was supposed to deliver.

We even found evidence that the FAA had actually ordered supplies without first obtaining prices. We knew what we were going to pay only after we got the bill!

The blanket purchase orders covering large amounts of supplies bought from a specific firm over a specified period of time did not even list the names of those at FAA who were authorized to make the purchases. As a result, an engineer knowing of such a blanket purchase order could simply pick up a telephone, call the company and order a dozen of whatever he wanted. The company would send the parts and bill the FAA.

The result was that for weeks afterwards clerks were scurrying about the agency trying to find out who had ordered what, and whether the merchandise had been received in order that the bill could be paid.

As usual, we found that some recommendations made in previous inspections, in this case three such evaluations, were never put into effect.

One would expect that after a report like this the entire organization, and especially the top management officials, would make extra efforts to clear up the continuing and serious problems in an area as sensitive as procurement. But that's not how it's done at FAA.

Our report, for example, was completed on November 11, 1966. That report was sent back to the Procurement Operations Division for their comments, which were provided eleven days later. Shortly thereafter, John B. Hogan, the director of the Installation and Materiel Service and my boss at the time, asked me to get together with the management of the division and, as he put it, "get on with the matter." My staff then made repeated attempts to comply, but to no avail.

By late January, after failing to obtain any action on my report, I wrote to Hogan noting that "seventy-seven days have passed and the matter is still in the stage of examining in meticulous detail whether our evaluation staff may or may not have made some minor statistical errors. Our report also included an observation with respect to the fact that quite a few employes of that division had offered critical comments about the division. We have been questioned repeatedly on the proposition that we did not validate the criticisms by the employes. We have made no attempt to do so, but did strongly suggest that the incidence of these comments should be of sufficient importance to division management to examine the subject and put it to rest one way or another." Obviously, the division management had decided to take the evaluators to task for listening to the work force.

Seven months later my report was still on Hogan's desk. I decided to find out why it had not been forwarded to the administrator, who was then General William F. McKee.

McKee was intensely interested in what went on at FAA. In fact, most of the administrators are very interested, but their top staff members seldom keep them informed. Some of the top career civil servants act as buffers between the administrator and the staff, providing the administrator enough information to give him the impression he knows what's going on, while at the same time protecting their friends in the ranks below in the event that evidence of poor management is uncovered.

McKee, however, wanted everybody to keep him well-informed. He went out of his way to say so. On May 1, 1967, while our report on supply continued to languish on Hogan's desk, McKee sent a memorandum to all service and office directors and all regional and center directors. It said, in part:

"I want to re-emphasize to you the need for a continuous accurate reporting to the administrator on the state of this agency.

"Under a decentralized concept, when delegation of authority has been extended far to bring management closer to the field, lines of communications are lengthened and subject to breakdown. For this reason, strong, effective headquarters, regional and area evaluation efforts are imperative.

"I ask you to carefully assess our effectiveness and factors that influence our services to the public in this light. We must assure that evaluations are frequent and meaningful and more, that findings are reported appropriately and any necessary corrective action taken promptly. By reviewing regional reports, headquarters can recognize national trends which might be corrected before becoming troublesome. Each regional and service director is held personally responsible for knowing first-hand the quality of services provided.

"To assure timely communications upward, significant findings should be brought immediately to the attention of the administrator or deputy. . . ."

My attempt to follow McKee's order and bring to him these significant findings won me only a little typewritten reminder from Clement E. Mayhall, who was second in command to Donald F. King, then director of the Logistics Service. The reminder said only that FAA regulations state that "an information copy of any appraisal report hereafter prepared in an FAA office, service, region or aeronautical center shall be furnished to the Office of Appraisal."

The Office of Appraisal is in the administrator's office itself, and therefore Hogan's failure to forward my report could have been considered a violation of FAA regulations. I say "could have been" because two months later —on September 6, 1967—Hogan sent me a scribbled note saying that as the report "was so long in the gestation and so much time had passed in the back and forth discussion, we have considered it an internal draft. Hence, no copies are to be forwarded."

I had already learned a month before, eight months after completion of our report, that the matter was being considered dead. Hogan had finally answered my January letter: "The recommendations made in your evaluation of the Procurement Operations Division in the September–October period of 1966 have been discussed with Mr. [Samuel] Rabinowitz director of the Procurement Operations Division, who is taking appropriate action either to place the recommendations into effect or to take alternate actions which he considers more appropriate. This evaluation and the discussions which followed it are considered by the director to be a closed case."

What had happened during those eight months was that I had really been down on King, Hogan and Rabinowitz to get on with these problems and find solutions. Tempers naturally got frayed. And in typical FAA fashion the only problem with our recommendations—when it was all over—was that we had made them in the first place. And of course since they called for changes they were bad. And because they indicated that something was wrong, they must be wrong.

King, as I have said, was the kind of person who always wanted to keep everyone happy. He would do anything (as in this case, permit violations of FAA rules) to keep Rabinowitz happy. And Rabinowitz was unhappy because our report reflected poor management on his part. So Hogan finally concluded that the way to resolve all the problems was to tell Rabinowitz that he could put into effect any recommendations he liked and could ignore the rest. And I was to be told that the matter was closed.

The matter, however, wasn't closed. It was to pop up nearly a year later and result in an internal investigation and my own vindication—at least temporarily.

CHAPTER VII

THE TELEVISO AFFAIR

One major principle under which the FAA operates is to refuse to admit it's been wrong and always to defend its mistakes. This is especially true in cases in which the FAA is being criticized from outside the agency. It's bad enough criticizing the agency from within, but criticism from without is unheard of. After all, the FAA is never wrong—at least you'd never think it was if you were on the outside.

Take the Televiso case, for example. On August 29, 1966, I was given an inquiry from the General Accounting Office, Congress's watchdog over the bureaucracy, which asked that an investigation be made into some charges levied by Televiso Electronics, a Wheeling, Illinois, firm that had lost out to Texas Instruments Inc., of Dallas, Texas, in competition for nearly $2 million worth of radar equipment for the FAA.

Televiso asked that the award of the contract to Texas Instruments be set aside for a variety of reasons which boiled down to a belief that the FAA procurement personnel wanted to purchase the radar equipment from Texas Instruments and had done whatever they could to insure that TI would indeed get the contract.

Televiso contended that somehow Texas Instruments was being fed Televiso's bid prices and was given the opportunity to lower its own. In its letter it quoted a section of federal procurement regulations which says that "whenever negotiations are conducted with more than one offeror, no indication shall be made to any offeror of a price which must be met to obtain further consideration, since such practice constitutes an auction technique which must be avoided."

The letter said Televiso "questions whether this regulation was complied with in its entirety. The reason for this allegation is the result of telephone conversations with Senator Mondale's (Walter F. Mondale, Democrat from Minnesota) office wherein we learned that on two separate occasions Texas Instruments was permitted by the FAA to revise its price by telegram subsequent to a reduction in price by Televiso."

The company complained also that some of its confidential information supplied to the FAA had "gotten back to Texas Instruments." It learned this, Televiso's vice president H. D. Von Jenef said, because several of its suppliers "have notified us that Texas Instruments was complaining to them because they sold materials to Televiso for a price less than that charged to Texas Instruments for the identical components."

Televiso also complained that FAA's pricing policy was at the least very confusing. At the start, the government simply asked for a fixed price on the equipment—Televiso's was $1,813,779.03 while Texas Instruments' proposal was $2,014,470. Then the government decided that maybe it could get a better price by requiring a so-called incentive price—a target price and a ceiling price. Televiso offered a single ceiling price of $1,932,118.28, although if the government paid its bill on time, it would provide a discount, lowering the maximum price to $1,927,287.98. Texas Instruments, on the other hand, offered a target price of what it hoped it could supply the radar sets for of $1,838,740, but set a ceiling of $1,931,990. Texas Instruments won the contract solely on the basis of its lower target price and its contention that it would make a smaller profit than Televiso—although Texas Instruments refused to allow government auditors to check on this figure.

Televiso also contended that the procurement was "mismanaged and, to a certain extent, biased in favor of Texas Instruments. Our reasons for this statement are based on the fact that Televiso had to submit very detailed engineering and material breakdowns which are not generally requested in a negotiated offering. . . . During the period of the audit, Televiso substantiated all costs on our formally advertised procurement because we felt there was nothing to hide, since our prices were legitimate."

To get an idea of what Televiso went through in its unsuccessful attempt to sell the FAA a few radar indicators, one must examine the chronology of events surrounding the contract—a contract, I might add, that the FAA wanted concluded with great haste, so much so that it specified that the equipment was required with "unusual urgency" and therefore there wasn't time to go through the regular procedure of advertising for bids. It simply went to the two firms already producing the equipment.

An earlier procurement for substantially the same item that was advertised—and which Televiso won—took only forty-eight days to award. In this case, where "unusual urgency" required the abandonment of regular advertising, it took seven and a half months to award the contract.

The chronology Televiso supplied recalled that the FAA issued its request for procurement on December 29, 1965. Five times during the next two months supplements were issued to the request, usually changing small items, and in three instances the date for bid openings was extended. That brought us up to February 21, 1966—the date Televiso submitted its response to the procurement request. Then the action started.

On March 3, 1966, Televiso submitted additional engineering data as requested March 2 by the FAA.

Four days later Televiso submitted a breakdown by item, labor class and month for the aggregate engineering labor hours submitted, also in response to a request by telephone from the FAA.

On March 22, Televiso submitted additional engineering detail as requested by FAA's engineering department, and additional information discussing the facilities the firm would use in producing the radar equipment.

On April 1 Televiso submitted additional diagrams and engineering detail as requested by a letter from FAA dated March 30.

Two months later Televiso submitted the engineering and manufacturing manning charts and a breakdown of material costs for items over one hundred dollars, once again as requested by the FAA.

Finally, on May 20, Televiso met personally with FAA officials in Washington for their first negotiation meeting, which resulted in the submission of more answers to FAA questions. A second negotiating session was held two weeks later, after which Televiso submitted a revised fixed price proposal which the FAA officials had sought, and also an explanation for the price differences between its first and second bids.

On June 29, Televiso amended its price to account for some additional items sought by FAA. A week later, since by this time things had been going so long, Televiso decided to extend the period of its offer another three weeks. When the time was up, they extended it again and then still another time, until finally on August 11, 1966, Texas Instruments won the contract.

Eight days later Televiso complained to the GAO. On August 25 the GAO sent the complaint to the FAA asking for "a complete report," and four days later the job was given to me.

Working with me on the investigation were Mathew Markotic of the general counsel's office and Eugene Slyman, one of our own auditors. It took us about three weeks to complete our investigation. What we found was that not the least of the problems revolved around the price for the largest part of the radar indicators the FAA wanted. These parts were priced at $59,201.63 by Televiso and around $63,000 by Texas Instruments. In view of the fact that Televiso was already producing this item for about $42,000 each under a 1964 contract, the FAA asked each firm to submit detailed cost data and then submit their proposals to an audit.

Televiso complied while Texas Instruments refused, and the contracting officer, Raymond Mulari, prepared a memorandum suggesting that the FAA terminate its negotiations with Texas Instruments. In fact, a telegram was sent to Texas Instruments advising the company that the FAA would not negotiate with them but that we would be open to offers at a lower price.

But for some reason, after some phone calls between Mulari, his boss, Samuel Rabinowitz, the chief of procurement, and Douglas Siegal, an associate general counsel, Mulari was ordered to continue negotiating with Texas Instruments even though we had no way of knowing the validity of their figures.

Our investigation also found several deficiencies in the processing of the contract. Among them were that despite the fact that the contract was let through negotiating on the basis of a "public exigency" which was so great that "formal advertising would not assure delivery by the required date of July 1966," we found no documentation that would adequately support the hurry. In fact, letters from the Navy Department, which was to use the equipment along with the FAA, indicated that it considered the purchase of the radar simply for replacement and modernization. That is, the Navy felt there was no great rush.

The refusal of Texas Instruments to submit cost data should have disqualified them from further negotiations. The fact that the FAA continued negotiations even after the contracting officer, Raymond Mulari, recommended

against such a course may have given Texas Instruments
a psychological advantage in later negotiations.

The fact that despite the rush, the contract wasn't
awarded until August 11—a month after the Navy had
wanted the equipment delivered—even though proposals
had been received the preceding February, "is a serious
deficiency in the processing of this contract."

Since Texas Instruments did not submit cost data, no
analysis could be made or was made of their proposal.
In fact, the summaries of pre-award processes submitted
to the Contract Awards Board included a number of
inaccuracies—all of which conveniently made the Texas
Instruments bid look more favorable than it actually was.

An interesting sidelight is that when the procurement
of the radar indicators was discussed originally, the
FAA engineers recommended that they be purchased
from Texas Instruments simply by modifying an existing
contract. But the procurement personnel felt that the
fact that Televiso was then in production of the same
equipment under the 1964 contract prevented such a
purchase from Texas Instruments without at least giving
Televiso a chance to bid. They recommended therefore
that the purchase be advertised.

It's clear, of course, that the substance of Televiso's
protest was valid; that there was funny business going on
at FAA; that there were unusual phone calls between
some people who overruled the proper conduct of the
contracting personnel who had sought to disqualify Texas
Instruments. We concluded that it was incumbent on
the government to cancel the award of the contract to
the Texas company and start all over again.

But the FAA couldn't accept that. What they had

expected was that I would show there was nothing to the protest. So they put in another team within days after our report was submitted, composed of the procurement chief Rabinowitz and the lawyer Siegal, the same two who had overruled the procurement officer in the first place. Naturally, their report was a whitewash of the FAA's poor handling of this contract.

On the key question of Texas Instruments' refusal to submit to an audit, the Rabinowitz-Siegal report said: "Submission of supporting cost data and holding of an audit is a general practice in a negotiated procurement. It is recognized, although this is not mentioned by Televiso in its protest, that the company with which it was in competition did not submit such data or permit an audit. However, this in and of itself does not require the government to eliminate Texas Instruments from consideration. . . ."

In its final letter to the General Accounting Office— which did not include the devastating findings of our report—the FAA, as usual, relied totally on the rule book. It pleaded that regulations didn't give clear and precise instructions, and the FAA weaseled out of the problem this way: "The contracting officer had required both companies to submit detailed cost data in the request for proposals. Neither the regulations nor the decisions of the comptroller general provide clear guidance as to the appropriate course when an offeror refuses to provide all the cost of pricing data requested," said the FAA letter, signed by Donald S. King. It noted that the Federal Procurement Regulations clearly place "an obligation upon the contracting officer to require cost or price data," but "does not state what the consequences are of an

offeror's refusal to provide it." The regulations say only
that in such a case the contracting officer should withhold
making the award of the contract "and refer the case to
'higher authority.' The contracting officer complied with
the procedure specified in this section of the regulations.
The agency's decision to continue to consider TI's proposal was made by the 'higher authority' to whom the
contracting officer referred the matter, the acting chief
of the procurement division, Installation and Materiel
Service, who had been delegated authority to act as
'agency head.'"

Ironically, the FAA's award of the contract to Texas
Instruments was based largely on the savings the agency
hoped to attain through Texas Instruments' target price
which was $88,547 lower than Televiso's price. The
irony is that the target price is only the price Texas
Instruments was aiming for. Neither this price nor the
figures that went into calculating it were ever made
available to the FAA for an audit to see just how accurate
they were.

Televiso's honesty and candor resulted in the loss of
a contract to a firm that refused to be open with the
FAA. Further, the mismanagement and apparent bias
within FAA were covered up because the General Accounting Office made the mistake of allowing the FAA
to handle its own investigation. And, in typical fashion,
the FAA defended itself fully—disclosing only that which
made it look good, and suppressing that which was
critical.

There is yet another aspect of the Televiso incident.
The final FAA reply to the General Accounting Office was
signed by Donald S. King, director of the FAA's In-

stallation and Materiel Service. Although King was a fairly high-level official, under normal circumstances he would not have signed a document such as this. It would have been signed by at least one of the associate administrators, a deputy administrator or, in most cases, the administrator himself. There was considerable discussion in the agency concerning who would sign the document, and it turned out that King was the one selected. The others apparently (and with good reason) were afraid to sign it.

The handling of the entire matter also would indicate that the General Accounting Office isn't always the tough investigating agency everybody outside the government —and most of those inside—think it is. After all, what kind of investigation of a complaint against FAA did the GAO think it would get by forwarding the complaint to the FAA itself? Did the accounting office really believe the FAA ever would allow an internal investigation critical of itself to be released outside the agency?

CHAPTER VIII

DON'T PUSH

In the early days of 1967 the FAA became quite appropriately concerned with the quality of the vast amounts of highly sophisticated electronic equipment it purchased each year. The spur to the FAA's concern was the tragic fire on January 27, 1967, in the Apollo spacecraft at Cape Kennedy which killed three astronauts.

The accident brought into the open a number of problems with the Apollo program, not the least of which was the question of adequate quality control on the part of the contractors and subcontractors who had manufactured the billions of dollars' worth of equipment the National Aeronautics and Space Administration was buying for the Apollo program.

As a result, our evaluation team was asked to examine FAA's quality assurance program. In brief, we found that it was inadequate.

The FAA has two principal ways to check the equipment it buys. Inspections are carried out either at manufacturing plants in the case of very large projects or, in the case of small purchases, at the destination by the receiving organization. We believed that the FAA was pursuing a realistic and effective program in its inspection of equipment as it arrived on board, and that by and large the inspectors permanently assigned to certain factories were also doing an adequate job.

By contrast, we found that the FAA had never developed a planned and systematic technique that would assure that the end item will perform satisfactorily in actual operation. This contrasts with simple inspections that merely determine whether an item conforms to the requirements of a purchase contract.

We recommended, therefore, that the FAA develop and put into use its own specification for a quality program. During our examination of the problem in 1967 we found that a proposed draft of an agency quality assurance specification had been prepared by the Installation and Materiel Service in 1965, and had been sent off to another office, the Systems Research and Development Service. Nothing much happened to it after that.

We recommended also that once a quality assurance program is set up the FAA make a concerted effort to enforce it.

We also focused on the FAA's force of inspectors who stood on manufacturers' assembly lines checking equipment that the agency had ordered. The FAA had two types of inspectors: resident inspectors, who generally remained in one place from one to five years, depending on the life of a contract, and roving inspectors, who were just what their name implies. The FAA had, over a period of years, made an effort to permit individual inspectors to remain in a particular geographical area as much as possible as a morale factor. But we found that "the virtue of stabilizing the home residence for the inspector is offset by the undesirability of the inspector becoming a 'company man,' and losing his objectivity. Over-exposure and possibly identifying with a particular company should be of more concern than it is to the Reliability and Product Control Branch [an FAA organization having charge of inspection activities]. We were advised by them the problem is minimal because the company will often change its project management personnel, over a period of years, or from contract to contract."

To correct this fraternalism, we strongly recommended that a system of rotation be instituted and vigorously followed "to assure that the unhealthy situation be avoided and not left to the chance of company management."

We tried to impress upon the FAA the need for a quality assurance program. In a letter to Donald S. King, director of the Installation and Materiel Service, I noted that the "FAA must take immediate steps to produce the design and quality equipment to insure the highest level of safety in the 1970's and 1980's." Pointing to the NASA Apollo disaster, I warned that "the consequences of an agency's [NASA's] failure to achieve adequate quality have been notably demonstrated in recent months. FAA should do everything possible to avoid a similar experience."

Our report was completed on August 15, 1967, and was forwarded to King the same day. He sent us a thank-you note and some comments on the twenty-ninth, saying that the report was being distributed to various parts of the agency. The key recommendation on setting up a quality assurance program, he said, was being "referred to the director, SRDS (Systems Research and Development Service) for whatever action he considered to be appropriate."

That was the last we ever heard.

We did try a number of times to prod King to take some kind of action on our reports. In fact, each month in our status reports we listed, among other things, that individual evaluations we had done were awaiting his action.

Finally King got fed up with that, and wrote a memo saying such a reminder "is unnecessary as when a report is sent to me I consider your action to have been completed and the matter closed unless I think it necessary to reopen or extend it. Further reports are, therefore, to show these items as having been completed in terms of your responsibility."

CHAPTER IX

THE GAO

Our group was not the only one that was uncovering faults in the FAA supply and procurement system and criticizing the manner in which FAA "regulates." While our investigations were conducted from the inside and therefore could be ignored most easily, there were other investigations made by outside groups which could not be ignored. Although the results of these outside investigations often were studied to death within the FAA, generally their recommendations were not implemented.

During 1970 and 1971 alone, for example, the General Accounting Office, which is supposed to watch over the rest of the government on behalf of Congress, submitted no fewer than three public reports and one private report highly critical of the FAA, its management and its regulation. Among the things these reports disclosed were that the FAA is really a democracy, in that if those it regulates don't like a proposed new rule, the FAA will abandon it. They also found that the FAA, in its zeal to dispose of surplus property, has been discarding millions of dollars' worth of so-called "surplus" parts, and then been turning right around and purchasing the same parts new later on. Also, although the FAA has had the authority for more than a decade to establish minimum mandatory safety standards at airports, it has never done so, and the FAA has failed to properly inspect production of parts critical to the safety of aircraft. Although agency officials had been aware of this lack of surveillance, they never had even determined the magnitude of the problem.

In connection with production line inspections, the FAA promulgates standards governing aircraft design, materials, workmanship, construction and performance. It also provides surveillance over manufacturers which it certificates as being capable of producing aircraft, parts and equipment. Such manufacturers are commonly referred to in the trade as production certificate holders.

But the GAO found that certain parts critical to the airworthiness of airplanes were not being subjected to production surveillance by FAA or by the production certificate holders themselves. These are "critical parts," defined by the FAA as those which do not have any backup system, and if they fail, their failure could cause a fatal aircraft accident. The critical parts not being subjected to production surveillance, the GAO said, are off-the-shelf items which are bought by production certificate holders and which may be suitable for use in more than one type of aircraft.

These individual parts are known as proprietary parts because neither the FAA nor the production certificate holders have design control over them, and the suppliers are reluctant to permit surveillance of their production by the FAA or by the production certificate holders.

Under these circumstances, production certificate holders are limited to verifying the functional aspects of these parts when they are received at inspection points. These parts may also be bought by an aircraft owner directly from the supplier for use in his own aircraft, in which case the parts would not be subjected to inspection either by the production certificate holder who builds the plane or by the FAA.

What are these critical proprietary parts? The GAO obtained listings of them from officials at the FAA Eastern Region Office. Three of these are the flexible propeller coupling used in the DC-7, the failure or malfunction of which could result in the loss of a propeller and engine power; the engine fuel valve used in the DC-9 turbojet, the failure or malfunction of which would result in loss of engine power and create a fire hazard; and the flexible drive coupling for engine transmission assembly used in the FH-1100 helicopter, the failure or malfunction of which could result in complete loss of power to drive the main rotor assembly.

In a memorandum to the GAO concerning just these three parts—not subject to production surveillance—the FAA's district office admitted: "Malfunction and/or failure of the above noted parts, and the resultant propeller and/or engine malfunction, under certain conditions, could be catastrophic." This showed the GAO that the FAA had been aware for some time that certain parts critical to the airworthiness of aircraft were not under production surveillance. In the past "similar parts have contributed to or caused accidents," the GAO chided

the agency, saying that "action should have been taken
to bring such parts under FAA or production certificate
holder surveillance. We believe that such action should
be taken as soon as possible and should not be delayed
further. . . ."

The FAA's production certification program is intended to provide approval of and continued surveillance
over manufacturers' facilities for duplicating aircraft parts
that have been included in aircraft, aircraft engines or
propellers which the FAA had previously type-certifi-
cated. "Type certification" means that the FAA has determined that parts included in a certain aircraft, engine
or propeller assembly have been approved by the FAA
for proper design and material and that the parts meet
specifications for safe operation. The FAA issues two
other types of aircraft certifications: production certificates, which are issued to manufacturers whose facilities
are supposed to be examined periodically, and airworthiness certificates, which attest to the fact that an aircraft
conforms to the approved type design (the type certificate) and is in condition for safe operation. Thus, the
FAA is supposed to examine an airplane and its major
components three times: in the design stage, during production and before it flies.

In practice, the FAA does occasionally examine the
manufacturers—and the inspections are sometimes rigor-
ous. It's what happens later that sometimes makes some
of these inspections considerably less useful than they
originally appeared. Frequently, discrepancies are somehow "ironed out" between the manufacturer and FAA
officials. One example was an engineering audit of the
Cessna Aircraft Company in January of 1970. Twenty

variances from FAA regulations were found. Cessna agreed to voluntary action to clear up twelve. Of the eight remaining items which Cessna did not feel warranted action, the FAA forced the manufacturer to complete only one.

Similarly, at Cessna in 1966 a host of discrepancies were discovered, some apparently minor, and the manufacturer declined to clear up a number of them. In some cases Cessna agreed to eliminate the deficiencies in new models coming off the production line, but declined to make changes in already flying aircraft because "there have been no in-service difficulties reported." Some of the complaints included electrical wiring which FAA inspectors reported could be damaged because wire bundles were chafing on other moving parts.

The General Accounting Office also has been critical of the manner in which the FAA keeps track of the qualifications of pilots. In April 1970 it sent to Secretary of Transportation John A. Volpe a report giving its views and recommendations on FAA activities relative to general aviation accidents and the FAA's procedures for issuing air safety regulations. It recalled that reports issued by the National Transportation Safety Board indicate that in most instances pilot error is one of the causes of general aviation accidents. In 1966, for example, the safety board said that in 80 percent of all accidents that year the pilot was cited as a cause. "This points to a great need to examine the preparation and training of pilots in the first place," the safety board said, "their certification requirements, the maintenance of their skill, and their being kept informed with respect to the potential hazards of general aviation flying. It would seem important to determine the reasons for the unfortunate errors of so many pilots and what can be done to prevent them."

The safety board continued to express concern, and in its report on general aviation accidents in 1967, the board said that "the pilot was cited as a cause, if not the only causal factor in some 82 percent of all 1967 general aviation accidents. This compares with 80 percent in 1966 and 77.3 percent in 1965. The continued upward trend in pilot involvement . . . re-emphasizes the importance of searching out and attacking the reasons for the tragic errors of so many general aviation pilots."

By this time, one would imagine that the FAA would have gotten the message and done something to show at least that it was aware of the problem. And, indeed in December 1967 the FAA did do something. That month, for the purpose of improving the general aviation safety record, FAA issued to the public advance notice of a proposed change in the Federal Aviation Regulations (FARs). This change would have required periodic flight instruction for student and private pilots having less than certain minimums of recent flight experience, and proficiency checks for certain holders of other classes of pilot certificates.

In issuing the proposed rule, the FAA said "there is no conclusive proof as to the percentage of general aviation accidents that might have been prevented by periodic instruction, refresher training, or proficiency checking. However, a review of the accident records shows that many accidents can be ascribed to a deterioration of basic airmanship and skills, and to pilots' failure to keep abreast of new developments and operational procedures." Although the FAA had no specific studies supporting this reasoning, the statement was based on general knowledge among people involved in aviation.

As its procedure requires, the FAA solicited public comments on the proposed change. The proposal drew five hundred replies from the approximately one-half million individuals who hold pilot licenses of one class or another. Not surprisingly, 80 percent expressed opposition in the form of generalized comments. Among the reasons the pilots gave against periodic re-examination was that it would be too costly and burdensome, that it would not help improve a pilot's judgment (which had been shown to be a factor in some accidents), and that it was simply unjustified. (Nobody apparently suggested that re-examining the pilots occasionally—especially those with little flight experience—would aid the public safety.)

Then, in January 1969, more than a year after it had issued the proposal, the FAA decided to withdraw the proposed change. In its final project report the agency said that "we did not at the time the notice was issued, nor do we now, have any reliable accident data to substantiate a finding as to the effect that the lack of a requirement for recurrent training and proficiency checking may have on the accident record."

On hearing this, the GAO immediately began trying to find out why, all of a sudden, after some opposition from those most affected by the proposed change, the FAA had withdrawn it. As part of its review, the GAO auditors tried to determine whether there indeed was a relationship between the lack of recent flight experience of pilots and general aviation accidents. The auditors reviewed data from both the National Transportation

Safety Board and the FAA. It found, not surprisingly, that in 1967, about twenty-six hundred accidents (42 percent) involved pilots who had only fifty or fewer flying hours in the make or model of aircraft involved in the accidents. The data did not show whether the pilots with low flying time were students or more experienced pilots who were changing to another type of aircraft.

In a review of FAA information regarding the 133 general aviation accidents that occurred in June, July and August of 1968, the GAO selected pilots who had a total of five hundred or more flying hours, but not more than five flying hours during the preceding ninety days in that particular type of aircraft. However, the auditors found that flight data available from FAA accident reports and medical records on the 133 accidents were, in some instances, incomplete or unreliable and therefore insufficient in determining whether a correlation existed between these accidents and the pilots' lack of recent flight experience.

The only comprehensive general aviation flight-experience data the auditors found was included in a July 1968 report sponsored by FAA and prepared by Ohio State University, entitled "Study to Determine the Flight Profile and Mission of the Certificated Private Pilot." The report was based on a random sample of about 1,200 of 209,000 noninstrument-rated private pilots, and showed that of the twelve hundred pilots about 51 percent had accumulated fewer than one hundred flying hours during the previous two years and within this same period, 29 percent had flown less than fifty hours. A significant number of the pilots, 44 percent, had no flying time for one year or more. FAA's safety regulations do not require general aviation pilots with extended periods of no flying time to have a proficiency check before flying again.

In October 1968, about three months before the FAA withdrew its proposed rule change, the FAA Aeronautical Center issued a paper that presented statistical data extracted from general aviation aircraft accident reports of more than six thousand accidents that occurred in 1967. This paper grouped the contributing causes of the accidents under three headings: actions of personnel, aircraft components/systems, and unknown. The GAO auditors used this data to prepare a table:

	Number of times cited as a cause	Percent of total accidents
1. Faulty flying techniques	3,445	55%
2. Mismanagement of aircraft	891	15
3. Carelessness and recklessness	1,054	17
4. Faulty preparation for flight	345	6
5. Miscellaneous unsafe acts	144	2
6. Faulty navigation	40	1
7. Undetermined	48	1

Unfortunately, the paper presented no conclusions as to the underlying causes of the pilots' actions that had contributed to the accidents.

The GAO, as is its practice, submitted a draft of its recommendations to the FAA administrator. The auditors recommended that he now make a comprehensive study of general aviation accidents with a view toward determining the corrective measures needed to reduce the

number of accidents caused by pilot errors. They pointed
to a major air safety study sponsored by four members of
the House of Representatives in 1969 that recommended
"*as a priority matter*, periodic retesting of all general
aviation pilots."

FAA Administrator John H. Shaffer, in explaining the
agency's view to the auditors, said the FAA had undertaken actions in four principal areas. At the present it
was conducting a study to investigate, identify and substantiate the need for improvements in aircraft and equipment. It had also conducted reviews and analyses to
determine the extent to which human physical and
psychological factors contribute to the general aviation
accident rate, and had established an accident prevention
program in its Central and Southwest regions. (In typi-
cally elusive FAA language, Shaffer explained that this
program was "aimed at improving general aviation safety
through improved accident prevention methods and at
motivating the general aviation community to increased
participation in safety activities." He also said that the
program had worked.) The FAA had also adopted additional rules for flight instructors and pilot schools to
improve general aviation safety, and it presently has
under way a project to amend its regulations to require
an annual proficiency check for all instrument-rated
pilots. (Since only about 3 percent of private pilots hold
instrument ratings, this would exclude about 97 percent
of private pilots, presumably those who fly the least and
are therefore the most dangerous on those infrequent
occasions when they do fly.)

Shaffer added that the FAA's decision to withdraw
the proposed notice requiring periodic flight instruction

and proficiency checks for pilots was withdrawn because sufficient flight instructors were not available, but he provided no conclusive evidence to prove this assertion. What the FAA had done was to make an estimate of the annual man-hours required to conduct the proposed program of flight instruction and the examinations of the pilots; it determined that the program could be accommodated if the work load was evenly distributed among the available flight instructors, that the geographical distribution of pilots and available instructors was disproportionate. The FAA was of the opinion that, as a result, many pilots would experience long delays and inconveniences in securing refresher flight instruction and proficiency checks, regardless of whether it was worth this inconvenience in order to save a few lives. As it withdrew the proposed rule, it evidently considered these lives less valuable than the pilots' convenience.

Even the FAA's proposal to re-examine the instrument-rated pilots came in for criticism from the GAO. "We noted . . . that FAA did not initiate this project until April 1969, some seven months after the NTSB recommendation [to do it], and had not progressed sufficiently by February 1970 to permit the issuance of a proposed change to the FARs [Federal Aviation Regulations]. In our opinion, once an area which affects the safety of air commerce has been determined as being in need of regulatory action, FAA should pursue such action so that the necessary changes in the FARs could be made in a timely manner." The GAO noted that commercial and airline transport pilots who carry paying passengers are required to demonstrate their flight proficiency at least once a year. And even the FAA's own pilots are required to meet certain minimum semiannual flight-time requirements and to perform proficiency tests every year. The FAA pilots, who are used to ferry FAA planes and personnel (among other things), must either meet minimum flight-time requirements or retrain themselves by going back to school, functioning as a copilot or passing a pilot requalification check. As for the half million private pilots, presumably their inconvenience came first.

It is before congressional committees that the FAA most frequently uses the excuse that it hasn't the manpower to accomplish its job of protecting the public in insuring that aviation facilities are safe. It was this excuse that it used in connection with another General Accounting Office report, this time on airport safety.

The GAO issued this report early in 1971. It noted that the FAA is required by law to promote flight safety by prescribing rules and regulations or minimum safety standards. It has, of course, established safety standards for airmen, aircraft and other related activities, but while the FAA has had general authority since 1958 to perform similar functions regarding airports, for some reason it has never established minimum mandatory safety standards for such facilities. The GAO set out to find out why.

For one thing, although the conditions at airports obviously have a serious influence on flight safety, the FAA had no program specifically designed to evaluate public airports' safety measures. It relied instead on airport inspections under other programs which did not have safety as a primary objective. These programs neither singly nor collectively provided the data required for determining the safety of an airport. In 1967, however, the FAA did conduct a test safety inspection program at thirty-two public airports and found numerous safety hazards that could cause accidents. Certain of these conditions had been unknown to both FAA and to airport managements. Although the test safety inspection program identified a need for greater attention to possible safety hazards at airports, and FAA official told the GAO auditors that the program was discontinued because employee ceilings established by the Department of Transportation had not permitted FAA to obtain the necessary additional manpower.

Although since 1958 the FAA had had authority to certificate airports and to set minimum mandatory safety standards for public airports, it exercised this authority only to the extent of establishing advisory airport safety standards. Compliance with these was mandatory only for airport facilities built with the use of federal funds. Although the FAA was not making systematic and comprehensive airport inspections for the primary purpose of evaluating airport safety, two of the agency's services, Airports and Flight Standards, had several programs that resulted in visits to airports and that were concerned to some extent with airport safety.

The Airports Service had its Airport Facilities Records Program and its Compliance Program. The records program was designed to obtain, maintain and disseminate to the aviation community information concerning available aviation services and facilities at airports. The compliance program determines whether airports built with federal funds are properly maintained and operated.

The Flight Standards Service had four programs: the General Aviation Airport Surveillance Program, which was designed to observe general safety aspects and note problems; the Air Carrier Station Facility Inspection Program, under which inspections were made to insure that airline facilities at airports were adequate for the type of service they were to perform; the Air Carrier Certification Program, through which airports are inspected to determine whether they are suitable for the types of operations planned; and the Air Carrier En Route Inspection Program, which involved inspections concerning the competency of flight crews and adequacy of an airline's operating procedures, equipment and facilities.

Of all these programs, the GAO inspectors found that only the General Aviation Airport Surveillance program appeared to have as a primary objective airport safety. But GAO inspectors found that in the two regional offices included in their investigation, inspections under this program "were not being made on a regularly scheduled basis, and that the inspections that had been made were incident to visits to the airports for other reasons."

Coincidentally, in the course of the GAO's review of the situation, the FAA issued two notices to field personnel concerning safety at airports. One, in February 1969, noted that a "significant number of public airports have deficiencies which are the result of continuing neglect and failure to meet the terms of the agreements by which they were acquired or developed. Moreover, there is increasing evidence that the deficiencies at these airports continue year after year without a positive effort by the agency to bring about their correction." In September 1969, the FAA issued another notice to field personnel advising them that a pilot had complained to the FAA about obstructions in the runway approaches at three airports. The notice said the obstructions had been previously noted during FAA inspections, but that firm efforts had not been made to remove the obstructions. In fact, the notice said, a review of inspection data from just one regional office had disclosed that forty airports had runway approach obstructions. The field personnel were instructed to try to obtain corrective action on these runway approach problems.

The FAA's own Office of Audit, in a report dated January 5, 1970, on the Compliance Program, cast additional doubt on the appropriateness of the FAA's reliance on this program to insure airport safety. The Office of Audit reviewed, on a random basis, the airport facility reports from four regions for 1968 involving 210 airports with federal grant agreements and found that 111 airports—or 53 percent—had runway approach obstructions which violated FAA criteria. The office, however, was unable to obtain from FAA officials satisfactory explanations why airports with these deficiencies were not placed in a status of noncompliance with their federal grant agreements.

The GAO found that the Flight Standards Air Carrier Certification Program, which is supposed to insure that airports are adequate for airlines serving them, had undoubtedly contributed to airport safety, but that this involved a type of inspection that was infrequently used. Federal Aviation Regulations require airlines to show that each route it submits for approval has enough properly equipped airports for the proposed service and for the type of planes the airline intends to use. In connection with these approvals, the FAA must inspect airports to make certain they fill the proposed needs. But, as the GAO noted, "approval of airports is not an everyday occurrence and, at the two regional offices included in our review, we found that Flight Standards [Service] had not made any inspections of this type in the three years preceding our review." Thus, while the Flight Standards Service may have made a comprehensive inspection when an individual airport was to be included in a proposed route, it had no program that was concerned with the continued adequacy of the airport after it was approved the first time.

The FAA's 1967 test program, during which it conducted safety inspections at thirty-two public airports to determine the need for a comprehensive airport safety program, came up with 1,026 deficiencies. In examining the thirty-two airports, it found that thirty-one of them had obstructions and hazards, and deficiencies on the runways, taxiways or aprons. It found that twenty-eight of the thirty-two had lighting problems on the runways and taxiways; twenty-seven had safety deficiencies in the passenger and public protection areas; and twenty-two had fire and rescue service problems and eight had hazards from birds. Some of these deficiencies, the FAA found, required immediate action and others long-range action. In its evaluation of the test safety program the FAA observed that conditions that could cause accidents were noted at airports, that some of the conditions noted were previously unknown to FAA and airport management, and that airport management and tenants were receptive to and actively participated in the program. The FAA itself concluded that the program should be continued with inspections of all airports served by airlines in depth every other year, and inspections of other airports in depth every third year. Follow-up inspections ought to be held every other year.

Yet, the program, which could have proven of immense value in protecting the public, was not continued. An FAA official explained this to the GAO auditors: "Employe ceilings established by the Department of Transportation were not sufficient to permit the administrator to obtain the necessary additional manpower." (The old FAA technique again, admitting a problem but calling it someone else's fault.)

In a letter dated June 11, 1970, Assistant Secretary of Transportation for Administration Alan L. Dean wrote the GAO that the department intended to implement the 1970 Airport and Airways Development Act by establishing an airport safety inspection program and prescribing minimum safety standards for operation of airports serving airlines certificated by the Civil Aeronautics Board.

One area in which the FAA had difficulty excusing its sloppiness was in supply and procurement, the area which my staff and I had thoroughly studied over several years. Supply and procurement also has been examined occasionally by the GAO, as when the GAO decided to look into a massive program under way at FAA for disposing of excess spare parts.

During 1967 the FAA declared disposal of excess spare parts that had cost about $9 million, and were on hand at the Aeronautical Center Supply Depot at Oklahoma City. The agency had stockpiled five years' worth of spare parts. The parts involved had been purchased for use in maintaining the FAA's network of air traffic control and air navigational aid facilities. This disposal was prompted, in part, by a 1966 presidential memorandum directing that inventories be reviewed and that excess quantities be disposed of.

The supply depot was a very busy place. During fiscal year 1968 (from July 1, 1967, to June 30, 1968) the center filled about 444,000 requisitions for spare parts that cost the taxpayers about $25.4 million. It had on hand about 126,000 items that cost about $40.7 million in the spare parts inventory as of April 30, 1969. In connection with reducing its inventory of parts to projected five-year requirements, the FAA had set up its computer which automatically declared parts excess by projecting past issue data to future requirements. In so doing, however, the FAA did not consider specifically the types and numbers of facilities and operations for which particular parts were needed, and the expected remaining useful lives of these facilities.

The GAO found, as a result, that new requirements arose during the twenty-three months that followed 1967 for significant quantities of spare parts identical to those which had been declared excess during April, May and June 1967. These parts had cost about $3.8 million. The GAO estimated that the newly required spare parts would cost the FAA about $473,900.

The $3.8 million worth of spares was declared excess only during a three-month period. For the calendar year 1967 the supply center declared excess spare parts which had cost about $9 million. Additional spares costing about $1.5 million were disposed of during the same year due to expiration of shelf life, condemnation or obsolescence. Thus, through June 1968, when the disposal program was substantially completed, FAA had disposed of spare parts which had cost originally about $12 million.

Where did these parts go? Presumably, most were sold through public channels to the highest bidder. But FAA records showed that $3.8 million worth were transferred to other government agencies. This, the FAA contended, represented a saving of about $1.8 million—this included $1.2 million which would have been spent buying the parts, $270,000 interest on the $1.2 million for five years, and $313,500 in inventory holding costs over five years. But when the FAA records were checked closely, it was found that only $663,000 worth of the $3.8 million the FAA claimed had gone to other government agencies actually went there. In actuality, about $3.2 million worth had been transferred to the Military Affiliate Radio System, an organization of individual civilian and military radio operators, radio clubs and military unit radio stations that are used largely for morale purposes—although the military considers them as offering backup support to its own radio system during emergencies.

The GAO pointedly stated that Congress did not appropriate funds for acquisition, operation, maintenance or administration of the system's individual member radio stations and therefore there were probably no significant amounts of funds saved as a result of transferring the parts to the system.

That wasn't all. The GAO had selected a three-month period—April, May and June 1967—as a sample period during the major disposal program for studying in detail, and found that during those three months $3.8 million worth of parts was declared excess. But shortly after the end of fiscal year 1967 "it became necessary to purchase various quantities of spare parts identical to those declared excess during the three-month period." By selecting a sample of items disposed of and items purchased, the GAO estimated that FAA probably had to spend nearly $474,000 to buy the identical parts all over again.

Part of the reason for disposing of parts it obviously needed was the manner in which the supply center's inventory system was set up. Under its inventory management system, items for which demands are uneven can be repeatedly purchased and disposed of. The supply center's computer is programmed to calculate for each item, on the basis of the preceding twelve months' and the current month's demands, the projected five-year requirements, quantities to be disposed of and the proper amounts to order. But there are some items that may be required only every eighteen months or two years—or at other uneven intervals. Thus, the way the computer is set up, these items are, in effect, missed—and stocks of such items are declared excess and disposed of, only to be purchased again later in quantity when they are needed.

The GAO also found part of the supply center's problem was a human one. Individuals were responsible for keeping track of between twelve hundred and nine thousand items in stock. Unfortunately, these employees had no idea what these items were used for, and as a result never reviewed the computer advice on what parts to declare surplus.

The result, of course, is that millions of dollars' worth of parts are being disposed of by the FAA every year, only to be repurchased again new, presumably at higher prices.

CHAPTER X

CONGRESS, TOO

Not only the General Accounting Office, but Congress itself has been highly critical of the Federal Aviation Administration over the years. Congress also found that the FAA was guilty during the 1960's of a number of poor procurement practices.

In a landmark 117-page report issued in July 1970, the latest of a number of critical reports, the House Committee on Government Operations recalled that in 1961 President John F. Kennedy asked the FAA to conduct a scientific review of the nation's air traffic control system and prepare a long-range plan to assure safety and efficient control of all air traffic within the United States. Shortly thereafter, the FAA issued the Project Beacon report, setting out the general guidelines for a modern air traffic control system for the FAA to develop and implement—a system designed to meet the nation's air traffic control needs through the 1970's.

In its 1970 report the House committee noted: "By

November 7, 1971, the 10th anniversary of the Project Beacon report, no significant element of the new air traffic control system recommended in that report will be in operation. According to the testimony of a top FAA official in hearings before this committee, 'our present estimate of mid-1974 for completion of the system represents a six-year program schedule slippage.'"

This slippage has allowed the FAA to virtually stand by while air travel booms. In the past decade alone, with the introduction of jet aircraft on a wide scale, the number of planes remained relatively stable while the capacity, size and speed grew enormously. During the next ten years air traffic is likely to grow even more. But these figures are for commercial planes. During the decade of the 1960's general aviation—essentially private and corporate planes—grew differently. The number of craft grew from about 76,000 to more than 133,000 with a corresponding increase in operations.

And the FAA? The FAA has increased the capacity of its air traffic control system only slightly—completely out of step with the burgeoning need. Further, there has been no significant improvement in the equipment available to the air traffic controllers—the individuals who are responsible for safely guiding through crowded airways planes carrying hundreds of millions of passengers.

The House committee found that the "FAA's inadequacies in implementing the National Airspace System [recommended in Project Beacon] have best been exemplified in its repeated inability to manage effectively its procurement operations."

One problem was the fact that the FAA needed electronic equipment which could meet rigid performance specifications—equipment that had not yet been developed. The FAA made the mistake of giving performance specifications instead of design specifications to the developers.

In January 1967, after intensive competition, FAA awarded a fixed-price procurement contract to Raytheon Manufacturing Company for sixteen display units for use in the en route system. These were radar consoles for use by air controllers. Delivery of an acceptable prototype unit was to take place in March 1968, about thirteen months following the date of the contract. The contract contained no design specifications for the production of the unit. Instead, the contractor was provided with "performance specifications" describing just what the FAA wanted the units to do. At the time the contract was executed, both FAA and Raytheon officials appreciated the fact that considerable research and development was required before a display unit with the characteristics FAA demanded could be produced.

As the House report says, aside from the International Business Machines Corporation 9,020 computers which were then in production, the display unit was the most complex unit in the en route system. In addition to the display capability, the unit also contained a computer Raytheon was to design.

As the House committee observed, "Raytheon, an experienced display manufacturer ultimately sought to meet the FAA performance specifications by combining several new and advanced design techniques in what might logically be characterized as a design 'parlay.' Unfortunately, Raytheon did not select a successful combination, and has otherwise been unable to produce a satisfactory prototype. Present estimates for delivery of an acceptable prototype now fall almost three years past the original date for delivery as fixed in the contract."

But that wasn't all. Because of modifications in the performance specifications, the contract price for the sixteen units has risen from $44.8 million to $63.8 million. In addition, Raytheon has filed a $39 million claim against the FAA—and the FAA has paid Raytheon more than $19 million in progress payments even though a satisfactory prototype has yet to be produced and the government, in fact, has not received a single unit of display equipment.

The House committee concluded that "through the use of performance specifications under the conditions described . . . FAA became 'locked in' with Raytheon's failure to produce a satisfactory display unit. After having made commitments for equipment production, it is more difficult and costly to exploit possible alternative sources.

"Thus, the success of the entire program was placed at the mercy of a single contractor. FAA developed no 'fall back' position and did not undertake any parallel prototype development on this or any other facet of the new National Airspace System."

It wasn't that FAA hadn't been warned about the dangers of performance specifications for equipment requiring development work. The House committee had given such a warning, for as far back as March 1964 (this report was made in 1970), the General Accounting Office said: "To avoid unnecessary costs in future development programs, we recommend that the FAA establish procedures requiring thorough program planning, the establishment of realistic project goals, and the development of prototype models or systems in order that areas of undue technical risk may be identified and eliminated before the production of operating models or systems is undertaken."

FAA's obstinate refusal to recognize these repeated warnings against the use of performance specifications, the House committee said, "casts an extremely adverse light on the qualifications of those responsible for the administration of the agency."

The House committee also hit at the FAA for failing to properly organize its own internal auditing group— one of the groups within the agency that checks on its activities and one similar to the evaluation group that I directed. In 1963 the House committee had established general criteria for organization and operation of the internal audit functions of federal agencies. These guidelines were designed to afford agency heads a more reliable means of maintaining management control over their operations.

The reasoning behind such an auditing function was spelled out in 1963 by the House committee this way: "If this myriad of governmental functions is to be run efficiently, if waste in the form of unproductive employees, unnecessary activities, and unjustified duplications in effort are to be stopped, those in charge of these departments and agencies must have the means within their own organizations for discovering and ferreting out inefficiencies and waste. Quite obviously, if the agency or department head does not have the means of pinpointing these trouble spots, then the problem confronting the President in the formulating of an annual budget is readily apparent. And, further, the problem confronting Congress from the standpoint of authorizing legislation, appropriating funds, and particularly in determining the economy and efficiency of operations, is equally difficult. . . .

"The head of a large executive department or agency must have his own 'eyes and ears' within the organization, responsible solely to him, independent of operations and with unlimited jurisdiction to review any and all functions wherein waste or inefficiency might exist."

Naturally, one would imagine that the FAA and most other government agencies would have complied within a reasonable time. But, just as naturally for the FAA, it ignored the House committee's recommendations—this despite the continuing flow of adverse reports from the General Accounting Office relating to various facets of agency administration.

It was not until July 1968—five years later—that FAA, in response to a GAO review, agreed to consolidate and centralize the internal audit. But even at that, the promised improvements were never made, although a directive was issued requiring internal audit reports prepared as a result of agency-wide reviews to be sent directly to the administrator without prior review by the associate administrator for administration. Previously, the internal audit function in FAA was completely subordinate to the associate administrator for administration —an official with the broadest management responsibilities, and therefore the official whose responsibilities would be most subject to internal audit reviews.

The House committee noted in its July 1970 report that it had recommended that internal audits should "not be beholden to officials in the agency whose responsibilities are potentially the subject of internal audit investigations." Experience suggests that subordinates cannot be critical of their superiors and guaranteed immunity from adverse reaction. (In fact, at the FAA anyone who criticizes anything is likely to suffer, as my own evaluation groups and I had found over the years. It didn't matter whether our own boss was directly responsible for activities we had criticized, we found out later to our regret. The problem at FAA is that because of its largely ingrown management, the upper levels of the agency develop a sort of fraternity. As a result, nobody can be criticized unless the critic wants to be ostracized and, as I was, forced out of the agency.)

The House committee found that in the case it had examined—that of having the internal auditors subordinate to the associate administrator for administration—the recommendations of the internal audit group during the 1960's did not always receive the attention they deserved: "As an example, in October 1965, the FAA internal audit group submitted a comprehensive report to the associate administrator highly critical of practically every aspect of the National Airspace System implementation effort. Many of the conclusions in this agency internal audit report coincide with those of this committee. Yet, little if anything was done to carry out in an effective manner the recommendations this internal audit report contained." I had discovered that kind of reluctance at the FAA within a few months after I joined the agency.

It was indeed ironic that the House committee also found that it would be a number of years yet before air control route centers and terminals would be automated. Bearing in mind that this report was issued in 1970, I could still recall one of the meetings that General Quesada—the first administrator—held with FAA employees in the spring of 1961, shortly before he left the agency. He had been invited by a group of us in the agency to a farewell luncheon. After the meal he gave a short talk and threw the meeting open to questions. Somebody asked him what he saw at his departure as the most urgent matter to be dealt with at FAA. His response, and I still remember the words, was that the most important matter facing the FAA was "the automation, or at the very least, the semiautomation of the control of aircraft."

That was 1961. By 1970 it still hadn't been accomplished.

CHAPTER XI

WAREHOUSING SAFETY

In early 1969 my staff and I had barely returned to
Washington after about a month spent at New York
City's busy John F. Kennedy International Airport evaluating the FAA's Eastern Region logistics program, when
a letter reached Acting Administrator David D. Thomas
from the director of the region, George M. Gary.

"I am gravely concerned about our present procurement procedures and the subsequent impact that equipment delays are having on our ability to meet the growing needs of aviation," Gary wrote on February 25, 1969.
"It is because of this that I am bringing to your personal
attention the enclosed regional analysis of the impact
of equipment procurement delays in our F & E [Facilities
and Equipment] program accomplishment," he added.

Gary urged that the administrator might "wish to ex-
plore our present programing and procurement practices,
with a view toward modernizing these procedures so as
to have equipment available on a more timely basis."

He emphasized, "I am convinced that equipment procurement is the 'key' to a successful establishment program. If equipment availability is timely and delivery schedules can be relied on, the regions can plan and accomplish an effective and timely establishment program."

Gary attached to his letter a three-page single-spaced analysis of the busy Eastern Region's "Facilities and Equipment Program Accomplishment—Equipment Procurement Delays." In his report he made no mention that his region had just been through an extensive evaluation by our team, so I assume his letter was written as a defense to show that all of the problems in the Eastern Region were not his fault.

To his credit, there was a great deal of excellent factual material in his report. Much of it was information we had uncovered. But his report—and our evaluation—are both worth reading, principally because what was found in the Eastern Region is conceded within the agency to exist throughout the FAA.

Ironically, while we were discovering that incredible inefficiencies in the region's supply system were delaying vital projects—such as installation of badly needed radar and airport lighting systems—the flight controllers across the nation staged a partial work stoppage, one of their major complaints being the outmoded equipment with which they had to work. The complaint was indeed valid.

Gary's report said the region was concerned about delays being experienced in delivery of equipment for facilities and equipment projects: "There are numerous assigned projects which have been deferred pending equipment deliveries. In many cases, this has caused critical operational deficiencies in the en route and terminal complex. Some of these deficiencies have been alleviated by the diversion of equipment from lower priority assignments.

"However, such substitutions have been virtually exhausted and the major portion of the establishment program now is almost entirely dependent on new equipment procurements. The need for such equipment procurement is evident.

"The aviation community, however, finds it very difficult to rationalize why it takes from three to five years to install a system or facility after congressional approval of the project. The region finds it difficult to support and explain the administration's position when there appears to be an inordinate time frame from project assignment to procurement and delivery of equipment."

Gary pinpointed the difficulties: The long lead time after project approval which is required by the Washington headquarters services for the development and award of procurement contracts began the problem, he said. The relatively long period allotted to the manufacturer for the production and delivery of these equipments was a major obstacle to the delivery of needed machinery which was complicated by the increasing number of delays being experienced by the manufacturer in producing these equipments according to prescribed schedules." Gary felt he was overly dependent on the manufacturers' timetables because of the lack of a reserve stock of essential equipment necessary for supporting urgent unprogrammed operational requirements. Although no stock was listed in accounting records for Gary's region, we found perhaps millions of dollars of equipment lying about in warehouses throughout the New York area.

Gary's report complained, for example, that it was "difficult to envision why it should take over one year to develop and award a contract for the MARK I ILS [instrument landing system] equipment, particularly since this was not a prototype model. In April 1968 the region received a project authorization for nine . . . systems. Present schedules indicate that the equipment contract encompassing these assignments will not be awarded until June 1969. Equipment deliveries will only commence in June 1970, and then, dependent on priorities, such deliveries will be spread over a one-year period.

"This represents a two to three-year time frame for equipment beyond the receipt of the project assignment."

Gary went on to lament that such lengthy delays are not unusual in FAA procurement. "In fact," he added, "experience indicates that the region normally cannot expect equipment prior to three years after project assignment, if new procurement is required. In some cases, it has been considerably longer.

"The administration cannot hope to accommodate, on a timely basis, the increasing demands for the improvement of the National Airspace System unless there is some improvement in this schedule.

"This situation becomes even more critical by virtue of the fact that industry has made it known that ILS equipment can be made available six to eight months after contract negotiations. Therefore, in effect, a private sponsor apparently can accommodate a complete ILS installation within approximately one year after making this need known and yet, in our case, the period generally exceeds five years considering budgetary, equipment and installation aspects."

Gary went on to discuss the complications of supply delays: "The increasing delays associated with the manufacturer's inability to comply with equipment and delivery schedules . . . not only affects our ability to provide needed services, but presents an additional problem relative to the effective utilization of installation and maintenance manpower resources. On the basis of equipment delivery schedules, the region normally initiates the necessary personnel and training actions to insure that installation and maintenance work forces are available to accommodate these equipments. However, as so often happens, no sooner are such plans promulgated when word is received that there will be a substantial delay in the delivery of equipment."

Gary placed some of the blame on Congress, which was granting only limited appropriations, necessitating costly and time-consuming reprogramming to correct the most urgent operational and technical deficiencies. But he noted that there was an immediate requirement for additional radar, communication and navigational aids, "which can be procured and kept in inventory." Without it, there is no way to provide for immediate improvement "of the most urgent operational and technical deficiencies."

The answer that was prepared and signed by Acting Administrator David D. Thomas praised Gary's candor and urged him to do what he could in a trying situation. "I agree that we cannot tolerate any avoidable delay in the administration of this important program," Thomas wrote, adding, "I am sure that in the meantime you will continue to make the best out of what must be a very trying situation, and I thank you for your initiative in recognizing that I would want to have your personal appraisal of such an important program."

Sometime between Gary's letter and Thomas's reply, our report was completed. On February 28, 1969, according to a note I later wrote to Donald King, director of the Logistics Service—and my immediate superior—I discussed our report with Gary and his reception was "excellent." This was surprising because the report on his operation was devastating—and not all the blame belonged to FAA headquarters or the equipment makers, either.

The Eastern Region extends from Maine to Virginia. It is one of the busiest regions in the FAA, ranking with the areas that include Chicago and Los Angeles. It had, when we examined it in January 1969, a total of 967 projects listed on the books for which $31.7 million had been allocated. The first thing we found was that 400 of these projects, worth $10.5 million, had already been completed—but no entries had been made on accounting records, so anyone examining the records would think the work still was under way. We found that of the 567 active projects, 383—or 68 percent—were two or more years old. Of this number, 332—or 87 percent—no installation work had even been started on them. Construction or installation, we found, was being done on only 53 projects—or 9 percent of the region's active projects.

The reason most often given us by Eastern Region's management was late delivery of equipment. Other reasons included engineering difficulties at FAA headquarters, change and delays resulting from policy decisions in

Washington, and the interference of high priority work which had come along.

In our conclusions, however, we said "the real root of these symptoms and causes of the gross delay and slippage in putting facilities into service is management's failure both internal to the region and at the agency home office to take the necessary actions in a prompt manner to eliminate or drastically reduce the causes." We could really find nobody to blame because "the management lines of authority within the agency . . . are not clear and as a result no one short of the administrator himself has the responsibility for getting the end product job done—namely, facilities in service on time."

These criticisms were relatively mild, however, compared to the shocking conditions we found. For example, of an inventory of $7.8 million worth of materiel, $1.95 million was "excess and unassigned." That means that no matter how long it remained in the region there would be no foreseeable use for equipment worth nearly $2 million. Of the remaining $5.8 million, we found that nearly $900,000 worth had been used for proposed projects on which no work was then being accomplished. But the remaining $5 million worth of material, which had been assigned to projects, we found, "lies idle because in most cases the projects themselves have had no work done on them in the last couple of years."

As if that wasn't bad enough, we found that there was "an undetermined amount of materiel in the Eastern Region which has not been posted to the accounting records. This statement is based on items that were physically observed and for the most part were still in the original shipping cartons." As we wrote: "Line item by line item search through the accounting records did not disclose their listing. All items of this nature are believed to have been received in the Eastern region in early 1967 or prior years. There is no way to assess the values of such unreported property until an inventory is taken, but it appears extensive."

A sizable amount of materiel that was distributed to the Eastern Region, we discovered, "in many cases has remained idle for a considerable number of months. As the resting time increases so also increases the possibility of cannibalization, pilferage, physical damage and deterioration. Storage difficulties are encountered and materiel is often transferred to different storage locations while awaiting installation."

As a result, when the equipment is needed, it becomes a significant task to assemble all of the material. "Some materiel, although still within a region, becomes lost through inadequate record-keeping procedures. In one instance, an electronic installation technician used two man-days of time trying to locate some radar equipment for the Westchester County radar installation."

Bulky equipment items require storage and since storage space is not readily available in government-owned storage houses, the regions lease commercial storage space. Then, since the commercial area is available for use other materiel finds its way to these convenient storage areas—and in some cases these additional items represent excess and surplus materials. This unnecessary surplus equipment costs taxpayer money just to store. One area, we found, had nine lease agreements, under which the regional FAA was paying rent to house needless surplus property.

Our evaluators found, too, that original project schedules are seldom adhered to. The few we found that were completed on time were largely the result of high priority treatment by both the regional and Washington management. Most of the projects analyzed missed their originally planned dates by two to three years! The reasons for this included waiting time for additional funds, problems with new equipment, major revisions in plans and inadequate management control.

Final project costs, we found, were almost always greater than the initial allocation. The worst overruns were in the air traffic control towers. For example, the initial allocation for two of these towers was $1.26 million, and by the time we examined the projects, the overrun already was $870,000. We concluded: "The consistency of the over-runs is indicative of faulty estimating practices on the part of SRDS [FAA's Systems Research and Development Service] and the Eastern Region. At least part of the error is caused by the two to three-year slippage in schedules and the resulting construction cost increase of ten to fifteen percent annually, and the willingness of management to accept unrealistically low facility cost estimates."

We found also considerable fluctuation in priorities of work. Every month the regional officials decide what priority each project will take. Active projects are generally grouped into three categories: Highest priority (very urgent), high priority and low priority. There appeared to be no particular reason for any of the ratings —and as a result we found that projects that were classified with a low priority had been moved into the "very urgent" category within a thirty-day period. In some cases, very urgent projects are later classified to a lesser priority. In this way, some projects just never get started— and we found that some necessary projects dating back eight years never had been started due to "higher priority work."

Our report was submitted to Donald S. King. Correspondence about a month after it was completed indicated that King had submitted the report to "the divisions in this service which have the specific responsibilities for action in the matters involved."

If action on this report was the same as action taken on other studies it was to be largely inaction.

CHAPTER XII

OUT OF THE FRYING PAN . . .

In mid-March 1969, I wrote to the then acting administrator, David D. Thomas, complaining about the lack of action taken as a result of staff evaluations of the agency's supply system.

Although I had already been involved with the FAA for about ten years, the previous fifteen months had shown me how impossible it was not only to change things in the FAA, but simply to get a hearing on needed changes. We had, for example, presented Logistics Director Donald S. King six plans for evaluating the logistics functions of the FAA. None of them was approved, and we had but a few piecemeal, new assignments.

Members of my staff told King personally that they had been unoccupied half the time since their assignment to the Logistics Service. Although we made several suggestions to King and his deputy, John B. Hogan, of areas that badly needed attention, none of our suggestions was accepted. And there had even been a seven-month period during the summer and autumn of 1968 when the entire evaluation staff did absolutely nothing. Hanging over our evaluation staff was the unfinished business of the midautumn 1966 evaluation of the Procurement Operations Division—an evaluation that uncovered serious morale problems among employees that were translating themselves into sloppy and inefficient operations. Hogan had told me that Samuel Rabinowitz, director of the procurement division, would "make such improvements as he considered appropriate." I was told by Hogan that he considered the matter closed, and that we were forbidden to provide copies of our report to higher management officials at the FAA. In fact, I was given explicit written instructions that my reports were to be considered merely drafts and that none of them could be released to anyone without Donald King's specific approval. We were, in fact, not even permitted to look at the procurement problem again.

In the months after the evaluation of the procurement division, our team evaluated the procurement functions of the Bureau of National Capital Airports (the federal government owns two commercial airports, both of which serve Washington, D.C.: National Airport and Dulles International Airport). Our report on the two national capital airports was still pending release in mid-March 1969—nine months after we finished our evaluation.

In fact, other reports on areas that urgently needed management attention at the highest level of the FAA were lying on Director King's desk up to eighteen months after we completed our investigation. Our January evaluation of the Eastern Region, which found things in a deplorable state, was in King's office waiting to be released in mid-March 1969—and I was ordered to provide copies to nobody, including the administrator.

On March 12, my staff and I met with King and Hogan to try to develop a work plan for the weeks and months ahead. We made several proposals, none of which was accepted, and the meeting ended with no decision. Then, on March 13, without any discussion with us, Director King scattered my staff throughout the agency on a variety of "details." At the same time, King told me to go alone to the National Aviation Facilities Experimental Center in Atlantic City, New Jersey, for a five-week review of the logistics and materiel operations of the center. The center, among other things, studies traffic problems involving airways, proposed routings and possible improvements in the air traffic system.

This was the second time in about a year that King had dismantled the evaluation staff. The previous time, Joseph D. Blatt, an associate administrator for development, ordered the evaluation staff reassembled and its functions re-established. King still bristled because Blatt had overruled him.

That same day—March 13—I wrote my memorandum to Acting Administrator Thomas, telling him about our findings and King's inaction in the preceding fifteen months. Thomas was astounded to see the content of the memo and just seven days later appointed a board of inquiry, headed by Harold H. Leeper, the FAA's chief hearing officer, to make a thorough investigation of the matter. Several days of private hearings were held in order to gather evidence.

During the course of the investigation, my boss, Donald King, wrote his version of the problem to Thomas. For the most part his letter was a personal attack on me. He accused me of not being a "team player" and of appearing to "derive great pleasure in developing issues . . . which he can use to explode as bombshells."

Parts of the letter are worth repeating here because they provide a good idea of the type of thinking that pervades the FAA—especially prevalent among its long-time employees. In discussing our proposals for future evaluations of other parts of the FAA, we had suggested another study of the Procurement Operations Division, partly because of the deplorable state in which we had found it two years earlier. King rejected the proposal, he said, because "three previous evaluations made in that division had resulted in disagreement and very strained relations between Mr. Ryther and Mr. Rabinowitz, Procurement Operations Division chief, who contended that the facts contained in at least one of the reports were incomplete, not conclusive, and that many of the recommendations were inappropriate." Apparently it didn't matter to King whether the supply system remained inefficient—just so long as there was no quarreling.

As to the complaint that our evaluation reports were not reaching the office of the administrator—as had been demanded by the administrator—King contended that he could not rely upon me to confine my "explorations and reports to those matters within the responsibility of this service and to keep them in the context which would be most constructive and form a basis for corrective action. Mr. Ryther's role, although it is obviously difficult for him to appreciate or accept it, is that of an employe of this service. As such, his evaluations are conducted for me and his reports are expected to be to me." In other words, unless the report of a team of five highly competent evaluators is thoroughly examined by a middle-management bureaucrat who was not personally involved in the evaluation, the agency administrator is not to see the report. Moreover, King arrogated the role of final authority over whether the FAA's top management should be permitted to learn what its inspection staff had uncovered.

The inquiry was completed toward the end of June 1969. I never did see Hearing Examiner Leeper's report, but I was told that it absolutely confirmed what I had reported to David Thomas. Confirmation of this was provided in a letter from Thomas—he was once again at his old job of deputy administrator, since by then John H. Shaffer had been selected by President Nixon to become administrator.

The letter from Thomas said the evaluation staff "in the Logistics Service has not been used effectively, and we can achieve a more effective utilization of the resources if the functions and positions now assigned to the evaluation staff of the Logistics Service are transferred to the Office of Appraisal." That meant my entire staff and I were to be transferred to an office controlled by the administrator himself. The transfer was made in July of 1969. Thomas added that the other matters about which I had complained in my March letter would "receive further study and appropriate action taken as necessary."

It may, of course, have been sheer coincidence, but within a few weeks the director of the Logistics Service, Donald S. King, quietly retired. A month or so later his boss, Associate Administrator Joseph D. Blatt, likewise quietly retired. In a couple of months King's deputy, John Hogan, retired.

The transfer of our staff to the administrator's office meant at once a small promotion for me, a vindication of my complaints, and satisfaction in convincing the administrator that his business had not been taken care of as he had instructed in the Logistics Service. It showed that the administrator had concluded that our evaluators were competent and that we had tried to do a job. So impressed was he that he wanted us in his office to help him with evaluation across the entire agency.

Of course, I would have been naïve to have thought that the move from the Logistics Office to the administrator's own Office of Appraisal would be the solution to all my problems with the FAA. I had been in the agency ten years and I was well aware of the fraternity and the private arrangements between top officials. And my new boss, Archie W. League, had about thirty-four years with the CAA and the FAA compared with about thirty-three years for Donald King. They were old friends who had been working together for over thirty years. I knew both to believe in the existing order in the agency and to be men of strong convictions—so I knew my reports might receive the same kind of reaction from League as they had from King. But still, the horizons promised to be widor. And I had hopes.

CHAPTER XIII

. . . INTO THE FIRE

The job of our group in its new setting was to evaluate how well the principal missions of the Federal Aviation Administration were being carried out, and to report our findings to the administrator. In short, it was much like the job of an army inspector general.

The importance with which the FAA itself viewed the job was shown on my official orders assigning me as chief of the new Evaluation Division, a position labeled "sensitive-critical." My job description said I would be "responsible for the planning and execution of a program for recurrent evaluation of agency performance on behalf of the administrator and other key officials." It said I was to provide "executive direction and leadership for a staff of evaluators who specialize in one or more of the diverse management or technical functions of the agency." The purpose of this staff was to prepare and present "briefings on significant problem areas which may warrant the attention of the administrator or other key officials."

At the start, there was some evidence of a new-found freedom in our transfer from the Logistics Service to the administrator's staff. Shortly after our arrival we discussed our functions with Deputy Administrator Thomas. He told us, in effect, to figure out just what we should be doing, and to report back to him with a plan of how we were going to accomplish it.

We started by examining the 1958 law that created what was to become the Federal Aviation Administration. We found what we were looking for in three lengthy paragraphs of section 307 of the law, among the responsibilities of the FAA administrator:

"The Administrator is authorized and directed to develop plans for and formulate policy with respect to the use of the navigable airspace; and assign by rule, regulation, or order the use of the navigable airspace . . . in order to insure the safety of aircraft and the efficient utilization of such airspace. . . .

"The Administrator is authorized, within the limits of available appropriations made by the Congress, (1) to acquire, establish, and improve air-navigation facilities wherever necessary; (2) to operate and maintain such air-navigation facilities; (3) to arrange for publication of aeronautical maps and charts necessary for the safe and efficient movement of aircraft in air navigation utilizing the facilities and assistance of existing agencies of the Government so far as practicable; and (4) to provide necessary facilities and personnel for the regulation and protection of air traffic.

"The Administrator is further authorized and directed to prescribe air traffic rules and regulations governing the flight of aircraft for the navigation, protection and identification of aircraft, for the protection of persons and property on the ground, and for the efficient utilization of the navigable airspace, including rules as to safe altitudes of flight and rules for the prevention of collision between aircraft, between aircraft and land or water vehicles, and between aircraft and airborne objects."

In another part of the law, an entire section was devoted exclusively to "Safety Regulation of Civil Aeronautics." It spells out in detail just what the administrator—and, by extension, the entire FAA—is supposed to be doing to promote safety. Given to the administrator is the power to prescribe minimum standards of design, materials, workmanship, construction and performance of aircraft, engines and propellers, as well as minimum standards governing other equipment that may be required in the interest of safety. He has the authority to establish rules and regulations and minimum standards governing inspection, servicing and overhaul of planes, engines, propellers and other equipment; the equipment and facilities for accomplishing this work; the periods during which inspection and maintenance must be performed. The administrator may allow private individuals to make inspections in lieu of those made by the FAA's own employees.

He is to make rules and regulations governing the maximum hours of service for airmen and other employees of airlines, and any other rules, regulations and minimum standards that he may find "necessary to provide adequately for national security and safety in air commerce."

This section also sets forth the authority of the FAA to accomplish its principal task—certification of airmen, aircraft and air carrier operators to make sure individuals, equipment and operators are all performing as safely as possible.

Finally, after considerable discussion among ourselves and our immediate boss, Archie W. League, assistant administrator in charge of appraisal, we managed to agree that the chief missions of the FAA are certification and periodic re-examination of airmen and aircraft; operation of en route and terminal air traffic control services; planning and development of the nation's airports; and installation and maintenance of navigational aids and communications equipment. We noted these four major areas as ones which we felt should be evaluated in a letter to Thomas. If these are the missions of the FAA, we reasoned, the administrator is doing a satisfactory job if they are being accomplished satisfactorily. And that, of course, was our job—to tell him how well he was doing his.

In our plan to Thomas, we said we believed that our new Evaluation Division "should not be characterized as a super-technical inspection organization, but rather should examine how well the agency is discharging these major responsibilities and how well each is being correlated with the others.

"We intend to approach these evaluations through work with the air carriers, general aviation, manufacturers, private training facilities and all levels of the internal organization of the agency.

"We anticipate that our report to agency management will reflect the condition of each of these major functions of the agency, outlining both existing strengths and weaknesses."

As a starter, I recommended that our first project be an evaluation of how well the agency was certificating airmen and aircraft—a study of the Flight Standards Service.

Our proposal, however, ran into hurdles from the start. Although we had been told by Thomas to develop our own program, we were responsible directly to League, and with my reputation at the FAA, League was obviously scared of what I might do and how it could reflect on him and his friends in the old FAA-CAA clique.

League had by then—the summer of 1969—been with the FAA and its predecessors about thirty-three years. He had started at the bottom and worked his way up to the highest levels of the agency. But even at the top, he had retained the narrow view of the clerk at the bottom. During his climb, League had become an expert at quoting the rulebook; he lived by it, and he knew it sentence by sentence. We were, for example, starting a new operation in his Office of Appraisal. Ours was to be the Evaluation Division, and its functions, he proudly noted once, were to be found in "paragraph 1211, page 68, of agency order 1100.2, change 43, chapter 12."

But when it came to something not printed in the rulebook, Archie League appeared at a loss. He never really understood what we were doing. He declined even to submit to Thomas our preliminary proposal for a work plan for the new Evaluation Division, largely, I suspect, because its scope was too broad for him to understand. League looked at the four major functions we had out-

lined as being the principal jobs of the FAA and noticed
that we intended to view the FAA from the outside—
working with airlines, fliers, manufacturers, flight schools.

"That isn't the way we do it. That isn't what we do,"
League said.

He was right, we later found out. The FAA indeed
wasn't doing its job.

But I finally managed to obtain League's agreement
to present the plan to Deputy Administrator Thomas at
a meeting. After reading it, Thomas commented that
this was certainly a new approach to examining the FAA
and its missions. But he agreed to it and said he wanted
us to "take a look at the safety function first, because as
far as I can remember we've never taken a look at
safety as viewed through the eyes of the consumer or
the user—be it the pilot, the airline, the flying school or
the flying public." And indeed we hadn't. We'd always
looked at the FAA from the inside out and never from
the outside in at ourselves.

Thus Thomas cleared the way for us to begin what
turned out to be my last project with the FAA, a complete
evaluation submitted to the FAA six months before the
Wichita State crash.

Immediately the six of us—my five evaluators and I—
broke into two-man crews and visited every segment of
aviation in the United States: airlines, pilots, training
organizations, maintenance operations, manufacturers,
flying schools and mechanic schools. We met with operators of hundreds of airports, with state aviation officials
in a dozen states, with dozens of our own FAA field
inspectors and with a wide cross section of the FAA itself. We spoke with perhaps 210 groups of people—more

than 700 individuals—in the course of a five-month investigation during which we logged a total of 150,000 miles for the six of us.

Each of my five evaluators was highly qualified in at least one segment of aviation. William Evans, a former Navy pilot who still practiced flying in all types of jet transports, was a supervisory inspector in a variety of safety fields in the FAA. Gordon Kewer was a seasoned air traffic controller who had learned where weaknesses lay, and what mistakes were causing improper flight operations, from his experience guiding planes from the ground. Richard Harris was a graduate engineer from Purdue University, who had been with the FAA about fifteen years and received extensive experience in engineering. Leonard Quiram and William Morehouse were both veteran maintenance experts.

We began our study in November 1969, and it wasn't long before we'd had a written communication from Archie League. To understand his letter, one must realize that all over the FAA at least once a year, top and middle management officials hold meetings and put on paper what's supposed to represent their division's plans for the year. Perhaps when this practice of writing plans began it had a valid purpose, but it doesn't any more. The high-sounding "goals, missions, objectives" are simply stuffed into a desk drawer to be trotted out when an inspector comes through. They're never used otherwise— there simply isn't any planning at the FAA. Most of these plans are, therefore, just pieces of paper—and that's what I called them frequently during our study of the Flight Standards Service. In his letter of December 8, 1969, League objected to my phrase: "In our discussion [four days earlier] we also touched on your interviews with division chiefs and staff personnel of the Flight Standards Service. It was distressing for me to learn that you have determined that the programs, the goals, the plans, the objectives, as they were outlined to you during these interviews are in your opinion 'just so many pieces of paper.' I would hope that in your project report you will indicate your basis for this conclusion, and if you deem it appropriate consider the advisability of an appraisal project to look in depth at this particular segment of the Flight Standards Service."

There were also times when League appeared to lapse into pure bureaucratese. In discussing our efforts to examine how well—or poorly—the Flight Standards Service was performing its function of certificating pilots and aircraft, League had this to say: "By concentrating your efforts solely on the certification function of the Flight Standards Service, you in a sense are going beyond your assigned function as outlined in Agency Order 1100.2, Change 43, Paragraph 1211, in that it appears you are conducting an in-depth appraisal rather than an evaluation, as defined in your assigned function."

League's comment that we were concentrating our efforts "solely on the certification function" showed that he wasn't really grasping the purpose of the agency— because that's what the FAA is all about: certifying airmen and aircraft.

League indicated his inability to comprehend this fact several times. Even before we began our project, League contended that Flight Standards Service did more than just "the simple certification of aircraft and airmen." We, however, were using the term "certification" in its broadest sense. He was using it in its narrowest term: the mere signature of some FAA official on a pilot's license or on an aircraft inspection report.

All of us in the Evaluation Division tried to show League that certification was the all-embracing subject of the FAA's business, that certification has to do with the qualification of a person or the engineering character-istics of an airplane, or the curriculum and instruction staff of a school. The certification of an airplane means certifying its engineering soundness, the process by which it is produced, its final testing and flight check, and the maintenance processes that it undergoes. Certi-fication of an airman includes certification of the school an airman attends where he gets his first basic flight training and the method by which he is upgraded to multiengine jets and instrument flight. So everything the FAA does with regard to people or planes is really part of the certification process. That's why we felt it was highly important and more than just a signature on a pilot's license.

Then, in mid-January 1970, when we were about two-thirds completed with our investigation, we received an-other missive from League. This was his formal plan for the evaluation we had almost finished on the Flight Stand-ards Service. It was, of course, too late to use League's plan, since the report was due no later than March 31, but the plan contained a noteworthy order: "Problem areas which become apparent as a result of this evaluation will not be explored in depth by the evaluation specialist assigned to this project. Such problem areas will be re-ferred to the Assistant Administrator for Appraisal

[League] by the Evaluation Division Chief [me] for decision as to further disposition."

Were we doing too thorough a job? Were we uncovering some things that League or his friends wanted left unsaid? Had some of his friends complained that what we found might prove embarrassing if it became public?

Our report, condensing into twenty-nine pages the contents of three filing cabinets, was submitted on the morning of March 30, 1970—two working days ahead of time. I handed it to League personally. The report appears in full in the Appendix.

We made dozens of recommendations, the most important one being that all flying schools should be required to have FAA certification. There are about five thousand flying schools in the United States, but only about two thousand of them are certificated. The other three thousand are operated just as loosely as the owner desires. In order to get FAA certification, a school operator must have an approved curriculum, a trained chief flight instructor, a facility of at least a specified minimum size. At present, the only incentive a school owner has for seeking certification is Veterans Administration funds, as the VA will authorize flight training under GI bill benefits only at FAA-certificated schools. Noncertificated schools can offer cut-rate prices, and many only have to certify that their students have had the required thirty-five hours of flight training to make their students eligible for an easy test given by a pilot examiner. The FAA certification would make certain that prospective pilots have at least some semblance of proper training.

We felt particularly strong about our recommendations

on flying schools. After all, the real heart of teaching people to fly is the instructor himself—and there is currently little or no control over these instructors. Many are poorly motivated, and most of them take these jobs merely to acquire hours in the air so they can eventually become airline pilots.

Many of these flying schools are operating on a financial shoestring, and are cutting corners wherever they can. Hundreds of times we were told by FAA inspectors that they couldn't control these schools because there were just no regulatory teeth with which to do it.

They were certain that many students were slipping through with insufficient training—and there's good reason to believe them. After all, often these flight schools have franchises to sell aircraft—and many of the inspectors who give the students their final examinations may well be airplane salesmen. It is, of course, worth noting that these flight inspectors are not full-time FAA employees. They simply apply for such a position, and unless there is something grossly wrong with them they receive it. Such individuals must, of course, be pilots and must demonstrate they can fly one of these little puddle-jumpers, and they must know the various maneuvers. Such an individual serves on a fee basis—he gets paid by the student he's inspecting (at the same time he's employed as a salesman for a firm selling the kind of planes the student may want to buy—a Cessna, Beech or Piper). This is akin to an automobile licensing examiner being a full-time automobile salesman and accepting a fee from a prospective automobile driver who may eventually become his customer. The possibilities for conflict of interest are obviously huge.

These designated pilot examiners, incidentally, are responsible for examining about 95 percent of all new student pilots. There is only a very small percentage of these students who have ever been flight checked by a government examiner.

Our immediate superior, Archie W. League, called our recommendations on flight schools "commendable" in his critique of our report. But he had this additional comment: "I have personal knowledge of many airports throughout this country of ours that do not have flying schools which are FAA approved which are training local people to fly who would not engage in flying if it was necessary for them to travel sometimes several hundred miles in order to get to and receive training at, an FAA approved flight school. . . . If we were able to make this recommendation stick, we would be in some respects stifling the growth of aviation." He recommended that our report be changed to suggest that either individuals be restricted to certain types of aircraft if they have not attended an FAA-approved school, or that they be "carefully checked by an FAA inspector before being given a pilot's license."

This type of comment is typical of the thinking at FAA, which worries more about advancing the growth of aviation than about safe flights. His criticism is, of course, ludicrous. There is no reason why in the smallest community of perhaps two hundred residents, a little airport with three planes and one flyer could not be an FAA-certificated flying school. We had envisioned that it was entirely possible—and certainly proper—that a one-man flying school could use an FAA-approved curriculum and meet the standards to have his operation certificated.

Our second most significant recommendation had to do with noncertificated passenger and cargo-carrying flight operations. Our recommendations here urged that regulations governing so-called noncertificated operators be upgraded to provide stricter controls over all phases of their operations. We recommended also an intensified surveillance and enforcement program. Had this recommendation been in effect, we might have avoided such tragedies as the crash that took the lives of many Wichita State University football players. Interviews with many FAA inspectors showed they were concerned over their inability to properly control or oversee the activities of noncertificated operators. These are operators who carry passengers and cargo under the very minimal requirements of Part 91 of the Federal Aviation Regulations (FARs). Qualifications of crews and mechanics employed by many of these operators are marginal, and inspectors, in an attempt to improve the safety of these operators, often devote an inordinate amount of time to their surveillance. Some inspectors said they had resorted to appealing to the better judgment of customers in attempting to dissuade them from doing business with operators whom they felt functioned in a potentially hazardous manner.

A third important set of recommendations dealt with FAA regulations themselves. We found that they are not up to date; they are unclear; they are unenforceable; they take too long to develop; they remain unchanged because proposed rules are often dropped because of pressure from the very industry that the FAA regulates. We recommended that the FAA review its rules at least annually, and that any new rules be placed into effect promptly. We found that even a noncontroversial rule change requiring no hearings takes, from inception to promulgation, an average 325 days. We also recommended steps to assure uniform interpretation of regulations throughout the agency. We found evidence that regulations are interpreted so unevenly that somebody who wants a major alteration to an aircraft may shop around among regions and find a region in which the alteration will be approved in a subordinate field office. Only some regions require that the regional office itself approve such requests.

CHAPTER XIV

MY COURT-MARTIAL

I suppose I should have been prepared for what happened after I submitted my report, but I still had a little idealism left. I expected that because of the seriousness of the allegations we had made in our report it would at least be forwarded to Administrator John H. Shaffer. But it wasn't. The report stayed on Archie League's desk for many weeks.

It wasn't that I didn't try to remind him of the importance of acting on its recommendations. The daily accident reports we received were evidence that something had to be done to stem the tide of fatalities; we were averaging nearly four fatalities a day during 1970.

League sent me a letter on April 14, 1970. He characterized our study as "basically sound, with few exceptions." And most of the exceptions he outlined in his eight-page letter were little more than grammatical changes, or minor rewordings. We acceded to most of his suggestions and returned the report to him.

Still, nothing happened; business went on as usual. Our staff and League were embroiled in another argument about our next evaluation. We finally settled on an evaluation of the installation and maintenance of navigational aids and communications services.

We had wanted to evaluate the entire airport system, but League felt that with legislation pending that could result in more than one hundred changes in FAA rules and regulations governing airports, such an evaluation would not be proper for a while. We then decided to evaluate air navigation, traffic control and communications services. But when he saw our plan League complained that it went "far beyond the original intent [of what he wanted us to do] and invades areas outside the function of your division." As a result, we all settled on the installation and maintenance of navigational aids and communications services—a plan far narrower in scope than anything we had suggested.

Still nothing was heard about our report on aviation safety. I felt that both Shaffer and his new deputy administrator, Kenneth M. Smith, were receiving a poor deal from League. With more than one hundred fatalities a month in general aviation, something needed to be done quickly. I felt that our report was being held up because while it named no names, it pointed a lot of fingers and the old CAA-FAA fraternity wanted it kept under wraps until the report could either be cosmeticized or watered down.

I learned that League meanwhile had given our report to James F. Rudolph, director of the Flight Standards Service, asking him for his comments, which was like giving the cashier an opportunity to change the auditor's report on his cash drawer. Needless to say, Rudolph wasn't happy with the report. In contrast to League, who found its contents basically sound, Rudolph said he did not agree with most of the findings and recommendations. He complained that many of the references and discussions in the report weren't current. He contended we were too vague, and cited as an example the fact that we quoted some interviewees as saying that "rules which are required to enhance safety are proposed and then later withdrawn." Rudolph said that for this to be meaningful "we should know if this is a single viewpoint of one of the inspectors or a significant percentage and what rules are involved."

Ironically, the General Accounting Office had just completed a review which dealt in part with FAA's procedures for issuing air safety regulations. A number of the GAO's findings were the same as ours. The GAO noted that in one case the FAA first proposed a regulation that would have required periodic proficiency checks for certain holders of pilot certificates, but then withdrew it after the pilots said they didn't want the rule. This GAO report was dated April 3, 1970, only several weeks before Rudolph wrote his letter complaining that our similar evaluation was not sufficiently specific.

Rudolph closed his letter by saying "in view of the wide differences I suggest a meeting between our appropriate staff personnel. Such a discussion might clarify some of the points and make the final report more meaningful." And might tone down the report before it went to the administrator.

Finally, on May 11, I walked into Deputy Administrator Smith's office and sought an interview. Unfortunately, he wasn't in, and I asked that he telephone me "on a very urgent matter."

The next day, when Smith didn't call, I wrote a letter to the administrator.

I wrote Shaffer: "I most strongly urge that you and I find time very soon to discuss the findings and recommendations which I made on 30 March 1970 on the overall condition of our flight standard business but particularly on the subject of accidents and fatalities."

I mentioned that I worked immediately subordinate to League, that I had a staff of "five highly competent people," and that we had begun the study the previous October "on our own initiative without leadership from one agency official including our own boss."

"In January," I continued, "we were apparently doing too good a job because League wrote me a memorandum and told me to stop looking at anything in depth but to just hit the soft spots. We declined to brush the matter off lightly.

"It is my opinion that we turned in a darned good report of the condition of general aviation including a series of pointed recommendations for change and improvement.

"I turned my report in to Archie League on 30 March— two days ahead of schedule. He held it for 30 days during which time he made a few minor changes and then referred it to Jim Rudolph where it has been for about two weeks.

"I feel that this delay of about six weeks on this extremely urgent matter is unpardonable and I would like an opportunity for a frank discussion with you. I know you are aware that the GAO has addressed the Secretary

[Secretary of Transportation John A. Volpe] on the same subject recently."

It was three days before I received any indication that Shaffer had seen my letter—but the day after I wrote it, I got a scorching note from League. Apparently, Deputy Administrator Smith had called him.

League's letter to me asked my reply in writing as to why I had sought the interview with Shaffer in view of the fact that our evaluation report as submitted to League "was not satisfactory." However, he had written only a month before that it was "basically sound with few exceptions." He also noted that the report "is still in the process of coordination with interested offices," obviously, to give themselves a facelifting. And showing his pique, League signed the letter "Archie W. League." It was the first time I'd known him to fail to sign a letter simply "Archie." There were, however, to be quite a few more "Archie W. League" signatures before the year was over.

League's letter was an obvious attempt to intimidate me. The administrator had repeatedly emphasized that any employee may make a request to see any FAA official at any time. League's anger, however, showed that while official policy may say one thing about employees seeking discussions with higher officials, FAA practice is something else.

On May 15 I got word that Shaffer had seen my letter. My original letter came back with the following handwritten message at the top: "Noted by OA-1 [FAA jargon for the administrator], 5/15/70, WVV OA-2." That meant that William V. Vitale, the FAA executive secretary, had shown it to the administrator, who apparently didn't have anything to say about it.

Disturbed, I immediately followed up on my memorandum. I called Shaffer's office and spoke to Ansel M. Winham, a special assistant. Winham said Shaffer was on a cross-country flight in an FAA plane, but that he would soon be contacting him by radio and would discuss the matter with the administrator. About an hour later Winham telephoned me and said he had spoken with Shaffer, and the administrator had sent the message that he had no comment on the matter.

My attempt to seek an audience with Shaffer was apparently too much for League. On May 20, he wrote me another blistering note—this time accusing me of two acts of insubordination: my attempt to see Smith and my letter to Shaffer seeking an appointment. League, who called his note to me a "warning letter," lectured me on the need for "the proper handling of matters of this kind . . . the channeling through management channels of the agency of such information as you proposed to discuss with them." Then he proceeded to forbid me to take up this report—or any other—with anybody outside the office: "Due to the sensitive nature of our work and the sensitivity of the contents of our reports, I expect you to refrain from discussing our findings or the contents of any of our reports with persons outside the Office of Appraisal without my personal approval." He closed with a warning that "further acts of insubordination will be considered grounds for more severe disciplinary action."

A day later I answered League's letter. In my answer, copies of which were sent to Shaffer and his deputy, Kenneth M. Smith, I reminded League that from March 30, 1970, when our report was completed, through May 21, the date of this letter, more than 170 fatalities had occurred in general aviation accidents. "It is because of my high concern about this extremely important matter that if even some of the 30 recommendations which I made had been implemented promptly and had resulted in a saving of even one of these lives, that I believe that any delay in the handling of the report is unconscionable," I wrote.

I added that "as the report indicates, and as I have told you many times, the vast majority of the recommendations in my report had their origin with the industry itself and the inspector workforce of the agency.

"It is only because I feel so strongly about this matter involving the lives of the general aviation flying public that I felt impelled to bring this delay in handling the report to the attention of the Deputy Administrator, inasmuch as I have pleaded with you, without results, to release the report for consideration at the highest levels of the agency."

My letter, combined with the earlier contacts with Shaffer's office, brought results. I was to find them out on the morning of Monday, May 25.

The day had started out with the usual routine of other days. Working hours began at 8:30, and at about 11 A.M. my secretary, Ruth Saghatoleslami, walked in and handed me a sheet of paper. "Mr. Ryther, here's a letter that you'll want to look at right away. It's from the Deputy Administrator," she said.

It was a one-sentence note requesting my presence in Kenneth M. Smith's office the following morning at 9:30. For a moment I was stunned. I called Ruth on the intercom and asked her to have the staff come in. My staff— William M. Morehouse, William Evans, Gordon Kewer and Richard Harris—had repeatedly queried me about League's inaction in light of the growing number of fatalities. They agreed that morning that League was probably trying to whitewash the report. They counseled me to, as Harris put it, "play it just like we always play it —hit hard and lay it on the line, Phil."

This was the way we had always handled matters in our shop: we got together, talked it over, argued if necessary, and settled on a course of action. The course they decided on was the one I would have taken: standing up for what we believed even if it meant losing our jobs trying to convince Smith of the importance of what we had recommended.

Monday night was a sleepless one. The next morning— Tuesday, May 26—I arrived at the usual time and we had our normal morning staff meeting, which was anything but normal. I remember that Evans and Morehouse in particular tried to encourage me. Morehouse said to me, "Stand up and be a man about this thing. Don't back down because of the threat of what might happen."

So, at a little before 9:30 I rode the elevator to the tenth floor and walked down the hall to Smith's office where his secretary, Patricia Hall, gave me a pleasant, "Good morning, Mr. Ryther," and added, "The meeting will start in a few minutes and they're all in the conference room."

"All?" I asked myself as I walked into Smith's paneled conference room. Yes, "all." There, seated at the polished round mahogany table was James Rudolph, head of the Flight Standards Service, to the left of the vacant chair that awaited Smith's entrance. To Rudolph's left was George S. Moore, associate administrator for operations. Next to Moore was Bertrand Harding, associate

administrator for manpower, and at Harding's left was
Archie League. There was a vacant chair between
League's and Smith's, and I headed toward it.

Moore, who was always a pleasant, gregarious chap,
shouted a cheery "Hi, Phil." League grumbled something
that sounded vaguely like "G'morning." Moore then
popped up, "You know Jim Rudolph, of course." I hadn't
met him although I had tried any number of times to
meet him during the course of our investigation of his
organization. But he always was "too busy" and chose
to have one of his subordinates discuss matters with me.
But we shook hands now. Then Harding arose and extended his hand across the table. "I'm Bert Harding,"
he said. "I'm Phil Ryther," I replied.

Harding's presence was a mystery, since he was not
involved in aviation safety—the only one present who
wasn't. But the mystery was to be solved within a few
weeks by a strange conversation with Harding and an
incredible threat from him.

We barely had time to start small talk before the door
at the far end of the room opened and Smith stalked
in. "I want you to meet Phil Ryther," League said to
Smith, who turned to me and held out his hand.

Smith had a sheaf of papers in his hand when he sat
down. He shuffled through them for a few seconds, then
looked up: "There are two purposes of this meeting.
One is [and he turned toward me] I want to know
why you concluded this subject was important enough
to bring it to this level and why you are so concerned
about it.

"And the other is, I've never seen this goddamned report and I'd like to see what's in it." His face broke into a grin as he added, "It must be *something*.

"Mr. Ryther, would you now tell us why you feel this was important enough to handle it in the way you did?"

I spent about twenty minutes on my presentation. I did not review the contents of the report and made no effort to persuade anyone about the specifics in it. My purpose was simply, as I explained it, to "get this piece of paper before the agency's management so they can assess it." We had made a number of findings and proposals which we felt strongly about, I concluded.

Then, turning to Smith, I said, "Mr. Smith, you have asked why I thought this was of sufficient importance to elevate it to the level at which it's now being considered. I've thought about this a great deal. I have superiors and I rocognize them fully. But I feel so determined and so concerned about the number of people who have been killed since I became knowledgeable through our investigation of the subject, that I just could no longer sit still and not bring it forward no matter what I had to pay for it.

"As you know, I'm a very senior employee. The fact I'm being paid thirty-one thousand dollars a year shows that I have been given considerable responsibility and that the agency believes I am worth such responsibility. I also feel that I have a very high responsibility to the American people. I have knowledge also that leads me to conclude that the management, in my view, should pay attention to this matter. But unfortunately the results of our investigation never were brought to the attention of management. As I've already mentioned, we've lost about two hundred lives since we wrote that piece of paper, and

I cannot rest until I've brought it to the attention of the
management of this agency."

Nobody interrupted me during my presentation—there
were no questions. As soon as I had finished, Smith made
the first move: "Well, let's turn to this famous document
that you're talking about." Smith then began leafing
through the papers on the table in front of him. "Where
is it? I thought I had the thing here somewhere. Oh, I
found it."

League interrupted: "Ken, you don't have the latest
version. Here's the latest." League then handed him not
the twenty-nine-page report that we had given him, but a
forty-two-page version that included both our material
and some additional trivia League had added. It was,
however, substantially the same report as ours.

Smith turned a few pages. "What do you mean by this
—the idea that the government ought to certificate all
aviation schools?"

I told him that we had spent a great many hours studying the schools and talking with hundreds of pilots and
operators of schools. "It was our considered judgment that
under the terms of the Federal Aviation Act, it is proper
that the FAA administrator certificate all schools which
would be in the business of training pilots—especially
with today's more complex aircraft and crowded airways."

Rudolph interjected: "Ken, this is totally unsound.
People have been learning to fly since the Wright brothers.
And they've been learning to fly in cow pastures and in
fairgrounds and they'll always continue to learn to fly
this way. A father who knows how to fly wants to teach
his son how to fly, and if we ever went into anything like

this we would be accused of limiting the American public's freedom to teach their sons or their neighbors or whoever they wish how to fly. And if we ever adopted a thing like this, it would just be Big Brother deciding who can fly and who can't, and who can learn to fly and under what conditions. It's unsound, it's impossible, it's 'unthought' through, it's just ridiculous."

Smith, who had continued to thumb through the pages during Rudolph's comment, asked me about our finding that because of infrequent FAA inspections, quality control efforts may be lapsing at some manufacturing firms. "I see you've got a comment in here about the quality control of the manufacturing of aircraft. You've got indications here that there's a company you found that was not following their own quality control practices. Who was it?"

"Cessna," I answered.

"Well, tell us about it," Smith said.

I recalled our trip to Wichita, Kansas, and our visit to the Cessna plant during which we asked to talk with the individual in charge of quality control. A vice president of the firm, I continued, "told us how concerned they were about quality, and that they'd set this system up in their company where on every Tuesday this special organization would just pluck an airplane off the line and give it a real wring-out, and whatever was found wrong with it would be examined and traced back to the proper department. He was very proud of it.

"Then I said I'd like to talk with the man who ran this operation. So shortly afterwards I found my way to this man.

"Well, he was in his fifties, nervous, scared to death

that we were there. We were those 'Washington men,' he
called us. I asked him to show us how this every-Tuesday
operation went on.

"He described it to us, and it sounded like the very
kind of thing that good business would follow.

"I asked him for the reports of recent inspections. He
got them out of the file. In one case he found there were
twenty-nine errors in production, two of them very critical; in another case it was eighteen that his staff had
found.

"We realized that such discrepancies would crop up
anywhere since no manufacturing process is perfect.
'Now,' I said, 'let's see what happened as a result of your
findings.'

"At this point his face became very flushed. 'Mr.
Ryther,' he said, 'I am so happy that you Washington
people are here. I have not been able to get any response
out of engineering or production concerning these things
that are wrong. But now that you're here maybe I can
get the vice president to insist that these people respond
to these defects that we found.'

"Several of the serious errors in manufacturing involved switches in the electronic systems—defects that
could result in fatal accidents if not corrected. But although this inspection team had found these defects and
pointed them out to engineering, production and purchasing, nothing ever happened. In no case on the critical items that this inspection had uncovered was there a
management decision as to how to correct them."

Smith didn't comment. He simply pointed to another
part of our report, which said the FAA was not paying
adequate attention to companies that were designing

and manufacturing aircraft under so-called delegated option authority. These are cases in which the government has given to a company a license to build, certificate and produce an airplane without federal inspection. We had criticized this practice because of the lack of government attention to these companies.

"How would you propose to handle this?" Smith asked. "We can't hire everybody in America. We can't put everybody on the government payroll."

"I don't think we should either," I answered, "but while the idea of delegated option to these companies may be quite proper, I think there is an obligation on the part of the government to see that those who have this delegated option are honoring it. And not just playing free and easy with it. You know, there are any number of incidents when our inspectors have gone to these plants and found flagrant violations in production and design practices, brought the matters to the company's attention, and the company simply never responded. Not only that, but the government never even pursued the matter."

"Well, we've got just so many people, Mr. Ryther," Smith argued, "we can't follow everything. These delegations have been given to these companies and they're responsible for it. We're simply doing the best we can." He shrugged.

At this point Smith opened the meeting to the rest of the group. "Anybody got anything else to say?" Harding, the personnel administrator, asked, "Would you tell me again why it is that you felt it important enough to bring this subject up to this level and in the fashion that you did?"

"Because, Mr. Harding, we've lost so many lives. And

we—my group and I—felt we had some ideas as to how we could stop this needless loss of life."

There were no more questions and Smith turned to Rudolph. "Jim, I want you to take this thing and give me a note in writing on just what you think of it." Then Smith turned toward me. "You know, Mr. Ryther," he began, "I've known Archie League, your boss, for many years, and I've always found him very cooperative." (Smith didn't mention just how League had cooperated with him. League had been head of the FAA's Southwest Region and had held the ultimate responsibility for inspecting aircraft in several states, including Oklahoma, where Smith's former aircraft manufacturing firm, Aero-Commander, was headquartered. Smith, who had just come to the FAA, was chief executive at Aero-Commander when League was regional director.)

"Archie has always been very cooperative," Smith continued, "he's always been a nice fellow and I like him. And this is something for you to have jumped out of line like you have." (At this point Smith arose from his chair and began pacing behind me—from League to Harding and back again.)

"And I tell you here and now, this was totally uncalled for. There is nothing in this subject that should ever have been brought to this level. And I'm warning you now that I expect you never to do this sort of thing again."

As he began his last sentence, Smith started walking past Harding, and by the time his sentence was completed, he was through the door to his inner office. The meeting was over. I got up and left.

It was eleven o'clock by then. I went back to my

fifth-floor office and called the staff in for a short briefing. "Well," said Kewer after I had finished, "the old CAA is still here, still in control." Yes, indeed, I thought, Kewer was right. It had been eleven years since the FAA was carved out of the CAA and the old crowd was still running the show.

Smith followed up the meeting with a letter on June 5 in which he noted my "concern for aviation safety," but said at the same time he could not help observing my "lack of knowledge and appreciation for the efforts presently under way in this agency to cope with and to resolve many of the problem areas in which you expressed concern."

Then Smith said that after devoting an hour and a half to my presentation at the meeting he "was not sufficiently convinced" that my report "was sufficiently urgent to justify bypassing the normal management channels and procedures of coordination in presenting your findings."

Then, like a parent lecturing a naughty child, he added, "Try as we may, it is not possible to keep all personnel in our agency thoroughly informed of the relative importance of the many issues which we are obliged to handle. Neither is it possible to keep all of our personnel informed on actions being taken to cope with our various problem areas. We therefore must depend on keeping our top executives informed, who in turn will be well prepared to judge the urgency of matters coming to their attention."

He closed the letter by adding that the FAA places "great confidence in our top executives to control matters of this kind." And he expressed the hope that henceforth

I would follow established procedures. "Not only will
this result in the conservation of valuable time but will
also result in more realistic and meaningful reports," he
informed me.

It may appear odd that a senior official of the FAA,
especially one who had only recently arrived at the
agency, would go to such lengths to express his confidence in a subordinate—League. But it is interesting,
too, that Smith did not enlarge on his relationship with
League that had spanned so many years.

It was known within FAA that when Smith was
chief executive of Aero-Commander in Oklahoma, Archie
League was director of the FAA's Southwest Region
which was headquartered in Texas, and whose area included Oklahoma. In this capacity, League was ultimately responsible for inspecting the aircraft being manufactured by Smith's company.

League had a large plaque signed by officials of Aero-
Commander that had hung on his office wall. The es-
sence of the testimonial on the plaque was that League
had given service above and beyond the call of duty of
any normal government executive to the Aero-Commander firm. League held that plaque in high regard and
on several occasions pointed it out to me. After Smith
arrived at the FAA the plaque disappeared from League's
wall. Why it had been given in the first place or why it
was taken down, we never found out.

CHAPTER XV

HOUNDED TO DEATH

The meeting in Deputy Administrator Smith's office continued to bother me in the ensuing days, but I said no
more about it and began work on the Evaluation Division's next assignment, an examination of the installation
and maintenance of all FAA air traffic control, navigation
and communication facilities.

Our evaluation plan called for us to start the agency-
wide project by examining in detail the Eastern Region
headquarters at New York City's John F. Kennedy International Airport.

So it was that on the morning of June 2, 1970, two
members of my staff—Richard Harris and William M.
Morehouse—and I found ourselves aboard an Eastern Airlines New York-bound shuttle flight.

I was seated next to Morehouse during the flight, and
I remember clearly that the discussion that flowed along
between us centered largely around what we were likely
to find at Eastern Region headquarters. It had been many

months, after all, since, as part of the Logistics Service, we had evaluated the Eastern Region and found evidence of gross mismanagement.

After the earlier inspection, George Gary, Eastern Region director, had written a lengthy letter to the then Acting Administrator David Thomas pointing out that while there were serious deficiencies in the administration of the region, they were the fault of others. Bill and I speculated half jokingly that we could be assured no matter what we found on this occasion, George Gary would be capable of demonstrating that if things were not well, it was somebody else's fault.

Bill refreshed my memory about the previous occasion, and mentioned that Gary was a master at conceiving a very plausible and logical way not to deny something, but simply make it so apparent that if it hadn't been the fault of all the other people at FAA, Gary's own situation would be in good shape.

We also recalled that many months earlier we had found millions of dollars' worth of electronics equipment, still in original crates and cartons, scattered throughout the New York area in warehouses, rather than being installed at airports and other facilities where it was supposed to be helping in the safe operation of the nation's airways. We speculated whether any of these problems had been cleaned up, or whether we'd find the same conditions that existed a year earlier.

The chatter occupied most of the hour or so that it took for the plane to leave National Airport and arrive at New York's LaGuardia Airport. By about 11 A.M. we arrived by cab at the Holiday Inn at Kennedy International and had already registered at the front desk. I was just about to be shown to my room when I heard my name called out on the hotel paging system for a telephone call.

I picked up a lobby phone and found my secretary, Ruth Saghatoleslami, on the other end. "I'm calling because Mr. League told me to read a letter to you that he has just signed," she said. The letter said I was to "discontinue any further efforts" on our projects in New York, and that Harris and I were to return to Washington immediately. The letter said also that Morehouse had been detailed to an immediate assignment at the National Aviation Facilities Experimental Center in Atlantic City, New Jersey. I was sufficiently stunned by the letter that it didn't register the first time, and I had to ask Ruth to repeat parts of it to make certain I had heard it correctly.

As soon as I hung up, I dreaded that a plan had been set up by upper management and that the FAA was probably going to fire me.

I returned to the registration desk, undid everything we had already done in the way of registering for rooms, and called my staff together for a lobby conference. "What the hell are they doing?" was Morehouse's first reaction after I finished explaining the details.

Harris, who never was vocal about anything, didn't speak for two or three minutes. Then he remarked, "Obviously this thing is the first step in a showdown between you and the agency."

We decided to have lunch before returning to Washington—but luncheon that day was anything but a joyous occasion. The hour or so was full of speculation as to who was really behind this latest maneuver. Both Dick and

Bill speculated on the possibility of the agency bringing charges against me. All of us had believed for months that sooner or later the FAA would seek to force me out of the agency because of my outspoken manner that impelled me to push hard for whatever I believed.

The speculation also revolved around the possibility that the FAA would find "the most urgent need for Phil Ryther's services in Nome, Alaska, on a permanent basis." This type of transfer had occurred before in cases of recalcitrant employees, and why it had never happened to me, none of us knew.

As League had ordered, we left New York immediately, and by four o'clock that afternoon I was back in my office. My secretary handed me the letter to examine, but I found no new information in it. The "news" was destined to arrive the following morning in the form of another letter from League.

I arrived at work the next day, June 3, at 8:30 A.M., the normal start of the working day. League was already there: he always seemed to arrive at work an hour and a half before the office opened for business. The letter containing the "news" was waiting on my desk. It turned out to be a neatly typed, complete plan for evaluating evaluation efforts at practically every FAA facility of any size in the world.

"The survey," the plan said, "will start at the Western Region where an evaluation staff reporting to the regional director has been in operation for quite some time. Evaluation efforts are also performed at lower echelons in this region. Area offices at Denver, Colorado; Salt Lake City, Utah; San Francisco, California, and Seattle, Washington, will also be visited and interviews conducted.

"Travel plans should be arranged to proceed from Seattle to the Alaskan Region for survey at the regional office level and from there to area offices in that region.

"From the Alaskan Region the survey team should proceed to the Pacific Region for survey at the regional office level and from there to area offices in that region.

"Travel to the Southwest Region with interviews at the regional office level and at area offices in Albuquerque and Houston, should be next on the survey, followed by the Aeronautical Center in Oklahoma City. Following the Aeronautical Center should be the Central Region, with interviews at the regional office level and at area offices in Chicago and Minneapolis.

"Travel to the Southern Region should be next, with interviews at the regional office level and at area offices in Memphis, Tennessee, and Miami, Florida. This should be followed by travel to the Eastern Region with interviews at the regional office level and at area offices in Boston, Massachusetts; Cleveland, Ohio; and Falls Church, Virginia."

To accomplish this work—which was to include transmittal daily of interview results (but, oddly, no in-depth studies, conclusions or recommendations)—I was permitted to have one evaluation officer, Richard A. Harris.

League's plan called for this massive project to be completed in two months: three consecutive weeks in the Western, Alaskan and Pacific regions; two weeks in the Southwest and Central regions and at Oklahoma City; and two weeks in the Southern and Eastern regions. The cost of the project—largely the cost of sending two men halfway around the world for seven weeks—was estimated at five thousand dollars: five thousand dollars of the taxpayers' money to be spent in an attempt to chase one civil servant out of government.

As soon as he arrived at work, I asked Harris to my office. After examining the plan, Harris commented wryly that we had missed by a degree or so in our speculation as to my future assignment—but the effect was the same: they wanted me out of Washington. Both Dick and I were in agreement that this was not a real project; it had been manufactured simply for the purpose of disposing of me.

I learned later the validity of our guesses. A close friend in the agency contacted me that same day and informed me that he had been present at a meeting the previous day which was attended by a number of top agency management. Among those present were Deputy Administrator Smith, Harding—the director of manpower—and League. The consensus of the meeting, he said, was that the FAA would design a trip for me so disagreeable that I would resign.

After Harris and I finished discussing the planned journey, Dick offered to draft the detailed plan as to how we would go about the project. But neither Harris nor I was destined to go on that trip. A day after we received the new assignment from League, Harris asked for a transfer. "Due to the nature of the assignment and the events preceding it," he wrote, "I have concluded that management relationships within the Office of Appraisal have reached a serious impasse." Harris had had enough.

The difficulties of the previous months had begun to affect me as well. My blood pressure had shot upward, my physician said, and I remembered what had happened to a member of my own staff who had been ordered on a field trip that involved many weeks in August 1969. His name was Erwin C. Ames, and he had worked under my supervision in the Logistics Service of FAA prior to August 4, 1969, when our work was exclusively involved with such matters as the procurement and installation of electronic and communications equipment, and the procurement and disposition of a wide range of electronic and general supply items. Ames's work was almost exclusively that of dealing with inanimate subjects and rarely, other than dealing with other agency and company personnel, did the subject matter of the work involve dealing with human questions. By contrast, after his transfer—along with our staff—to the Office of Appraisal, which was run by League, on August 4, 1969, his work involved dealing with a rather explosive and highly controversial employee management question.

Ames was appointed a member of a two-man team which was to travel throughout the country working with FAA controller personnel in an effort to identify those matters on the minds of these flight controllers which had caused a serious work slowdown in the months before. Ames began his assignment about a week after his transfer and appointment to the new position. He worked long and erratic hours in his new assignment in an effort to meet with controller groups on each of their three shifts. This necessitated a very much broken-up work schedule and sleeping and awakening and returning to work as often as three times each twenty-four hours.

Although he was basically qualified for this type of work from an educational standpoint, his experience dealing with logistics matters had not prepared him well for the abrupt change to that involving highly emotional problems. When I asked him to become a member of one of the teams and take on the assignment, he said that of course he would adapt as quickly as he could—and he tried indeed. But he told me that traveling and being away from his family was personally a very distasteful proposition. However, the matter wasn't discussed further, and Ames accepted his responsibility and departed on the trip, from which he did not return alive. At the time he left it was anticipated that he would be gone for two or three months.

During the last year that he was assigned to the Logistics Service of the FAA, Ames underwent almost continuously disagreeable work experiences. His other associates, including myself, had a similarly bad time of it. On at least two occasions, though, Ames really suffered.

The first incident began about three months before his death. Ames came into my office, and told me that Deputy Director Hogan had called him into his office and told him he was not satisfied with his work. Hogan said he was going to downgrade Ames one or two grades (from a GS 15 to a 13 or 14) and put him in a different assignment to see if Ames could prove himself. The action was taken on Hogan's part even though I had recently given Ames a high efficiency report and Hogan had endorsed it without change. Further, even though I was Ames's supervisor, Hogan never told me about his intention. Ames told me he had informed Hogan he would have to think the matter over. When he related the story to me, Ames was pale and visibly upset.

The second incident occurred when, as a result of an official agency board of inquiry concerning the untenable conditions in the Logistics Service, the deputy administrator of the agency decided to transfer me and my entire staff to his office. He made this decision about July 1, 1969, and I was personally transferred five days later. For reasons unknown to the rest of the staff, they were directed by King to remain in their existing positions in the Logistics Service. This state of uncertainty prevailed about a month until the matter was brought to the deputy administrator's attention and he transferred the remainder of the staff within the hour. During this period of uncertainty, namely between July 1 and August 4, three of the five staff members were informed by King and Hogan that they would be given new assignments. Ames and the other employees were informed by King that there was no position for them and that they were on their own to seek other employment. At the time Ames was told this, he came to me and informed me of what had happened, noticeably shaken. He said he wasn't sure what he could do about it, but that he felt that it was a terribly unfair way of being treated after twenty-five years of federal service of the highest order. On this occasion, as on the first, he was pale in appearance and I asked him if he didn't believe he should go home for a day or so and rest. He declined my suggestion and remained on the job.

Erwin Ames suffered a fatal heart attack on August 18, 1969, while at work on a field trip for the FAA. He was forty-eight years old.

I decided that pressures were being built up within me, and visited my physician the very afternoon I received League's trip proposal. My physician recommended that because of my "general condition," and especially my elevated blood pressure, that I not be allowed to go on such a trip.

League backed down, but immediately began casting about for another way to force me out of the FAA.

CHAPTER XVI

QUIT OR BE FIRED

Having failed in my attempts to interest top FAA officials in the results of our aviation safety report, I decided that perhaps an appeal to the agency's parent, the
Department of Transportation, might help.

I should have known better, but I began with a letter
to James M. Beggs, undersecretary of DOT. Although
Secretary John A. Volpe was head of the department, it
was widely known within DOT that Volpe was there
strictly for political reasons and that Beggs, the "general
manager," really ran the department.

My two-and-a-half-page letter began with a recital of
who I was and what was my job in the FAA. I recounted
how during the autumn of 1969 I was directed to make
an agency-wide evaluation of the Flight Standards programs embracing the operation and maintenance of all
civil aviation, the manufacture of civil aviation aircraft,
and the training and licensing of all airmen engaged in
civil aviation.

The report of our evaluation, I recalled, had been submitted to Archie League on March 30, 1970. "It included a candid and forthright statement of conditions as we found them and 30 concrete recommendations for change and improvement in agency policies and practices," the letter said. I pointed out also that the vast majority of these recommendations had had their origin within the aviation industry and among the inspector work force of the FAA.

"The report was held up nearly two months by my superior, Mr. League, during which time approximately 200 fatalities occurred in the general aviation industry of our nation. During this two-month period, I urged Mr. League many times to put the report before the top agency management for review and prompt implementation of those recommendations found to be appropriate. Twice during this long delay Mr. League told me in writing that the contents of my report were basically sound," I wrote.

The letter to Beggs recounted the meeting in Smith's office and the events that followed—the dispersal of my staff and the proposed trip.

"I have been told that a meeting was held by several high officials of the FAA on 2 June 1970, at which time it was decided to design a trip for Mr. Ryther that would be so disagreeable that he would resign," I wrote, adding: "If this is considered appropriate disposition of me as a career government employee because I have been unwilling to turn my head from the manner in which aviation safety is being administered in this agency, then I have been misjudged.

"I expect to exercise every honorable means at my

disposal to prevent my career from being ruined. . . . I have been told in writing that I must not under any conditions discuss the findings and recommendations in the report I have referred to . . . and that if I should do so, severe disciplinary action will be taken against me."

I appealed to Beggs to at least examine the work our evaluation team had put together. ". . . the crux of the matter is the manner in which the aviation safety program is being administered by the FAA," I added.

I personally handed the letter to Beggs's special assistant, Frank Coy, who read it and walked immediately into Beggs's office and handed it to him. That was the last I heard of the letter.

Four days later, on June 8, 1970, I received a phone call at 3:20 in the afternoon. "Phil," said the voice on the other end, "this is Bert Harding, I wonder if you can drop by a minute."

Five minutes later I was in his office. It was only the second time I had ever met the man—the first time was a few days previous at what I've come to call Deputy Administrator Smith's court-martial of Phil Ryther.

"How will you take your coffee, Phil?" Harding asked, leaning back in his high-backed swivel chair. "Cream only," I answered. During the two or three minutes that it took for Harding's secretary, Carolyn Snowden, to get the coffee, I had a chance to examine Harding. The man looked about fifty-five, was about six feet tall, weighed about 190 or so and laid claim to having been an athlete. At one point, in fact, he leaned toward his desk and winced: "Ow, that old football knee." His ruddy complexion lent credence to some residual outdoor interest.

Miss Snowden arrived with our coffee. (I don't know

quite where she got it, but probably from one of the literally hundreds of coffee dispensers in offices throughout the FAA building. There must be thousands of these unauthorized coffee bars throughout government, each one requiring several hundred watts of electric power, and all perking away the kilowatt hours at taxpayer expense.)

When Harding's secretary had placed the coffee in front of us, he leaned back and said, "Phil, I've volunteered to be a friend of the court in this matter." ("Court?" I wondered? Then Smith's meeting had been a sort of court-martial—or at least a preliminary hearing leading to a trial!)

"I've been giving a great deal of thought to this matter," Harding continued. "Say, I believe you own a real-estate business, don't you?"

"Yes, I do," I answered. It was fairly common knowledge around the office that I had been involved in selling real estate in my spare time for several years.

"How's business going?" Harding asked. "I've known so many people who've been a success in real estate. How's your business?"

"All right." I shrugged.

Obviously, Harding was after a dollar-and-cents answer. He bristled noticeably and said: "Don't play games with me, because I can turn right around to that telephone and in five minutes I can know exactly how you're doing through your income-tax records from the Internal Revenue Service."

That was a blow. I didn't know my tax records were available to any government official just for the asking. Then I recalled that Harding had served as an assistant commissioner of internal revenue, so it really wasn't an empty threat.

I said nothing, shocked as I was. I felt the best way to deal with such a startling threat was not to show my feelings. So I remained calm and made no comment.

Harding's outburst took only a few seconds. Then he settled down again to being friendly.

"Phil, I'm here to tell you about some of the tax advantages that can be yours with all the service you have —twenty-six years, in fact—if you were to retire now and go into full pursuit of your desires in real estate and take an immediate federal annuity. There are three ways we can do this.

"First, we can do it on a compatibility basis, in which case all you need to do is request of the President your retirement, and we'll approve it, and it will go into effect."

Compatibility means simply that if you and your superior decide that you cannot get along together, and you have enough time in the government to qualify for retirement, you can obtain a separation from the government and begin drawing an annuity. Harding doubtless was well familiar with this course since he had retired from the Internal Revenue Service under similar conditions just months before.

"Or," he continued, "we could abolish your job and then you'll just be free to ask for retirement, because you'll no longer have a position. And we'll approve it and you'll be on your way.

"Now, of course, if you don't like either of these alternatives, we have a third—and it's not a very comfortable choice, Phil. Because if you decide not to retire we are prepared to bring charges against you. That would be unfortunate, of course, because it would cost you an exorbitant amount of money and it would be very expensive for you—and it would be a long and nasty business for all concerned. Do you understand?"

"Yes, I understand," I answered.

"Well, what would you like to do?"

"Bert, I frankly have absolutely no interest in any of your alternatives."

"Now don't be hasty, Phil, don't be hasty. Don't close your options. I'd like to have you take a little time to think about this. You know, you claim to be a businessman, and businessmen never close all their options."

"All right, Bert, I'll give it some thought. I'll let you know in about a month."

"Oh, now wait a minute, Phil. I haven't any intention of letting things drag on that long. I'll need to know in a week."

I agreed and we parted—each with a smile on his face.

That was June 8, 1970. The following day I sent an updating letter to Beggs. Although it had been five days since my last note (which ran to three single-spaced typewritten pages), and I hadn't had any answer, I decided to write again anyway. After all, I felt that he ought to know just how some of the officials in his department were conducting the agency's business—namely, threatening disclosure of an employee's private federal income-tax return in order to force him into retirement.

"I made no comment concerning Mr. Harding's assertion that he had such easy access to my personal tax records," I wrote to Beggs, "but I certainly have the understanding that such records are privileged and not available to someone who may want to casually browse

through them. I take great exception to the implied
threat to my personal affairs that Mr. Harding's comment
indicates."

The letter generally reviewed the discussion in Harding's office, although it did not ask Beggs to take any
specific action. I merely mentioned that while Harding
and others in the FAA wanted to force me into retirement, I wasn't about to go willingly.

Shortly after my second letter to Beggs I received a
telephone call from William S. Heffelfinger, a deputy
assistant secretary of transportation. "Mr. Ryther," he
said, "under no circumstances are you going to be fired.
The undersecretary [Beggs] has called me and asked that
I tell you that the conditions reflected in your June 4
letter are to be personally investigated by Mr. Shaffer."

Heffelfinger said that I should rest assured that Beggs
was happy to have an employee like myself in the Department of Transportation and I should understand that
"under no circumstances" was anything going to happen
to me. And, Heffelfinger added, "I am instructed to discuss with you what you would like to do. Would you
like to stay in the FAA? Come to the Secretary's office
to work? Go to another part of the Department of Transportation?"

I told Heffelfinger that I was pleased and grateful and
that I would let him know in about a week. Several days
later I went to visit Heffelfinger. I told him I had another
suggestion: that I should be granted a trial retirement.
Such trial retirements had been authorized by both the
Air Force and the Department of Agriculture, and are
just what their title implies. They allow an employee to
try retirement for six months or a year and, if he wants

after that period to return to work, he is given his old job at the same pay as which he left.

Within a day or two Heffelfinger telephoned me and said that Beggs had agreed with the idea, and it would be approved by the department.

After I had thought about this option for a couple of days, I decided that my currently heavy expenses—about eight thousand dollars a year for a son and daughter in college, not to mention some unusually large medical expenses—would make me forgo even a trial retirement.

Surprisingly, Heffelfinger consented. "That's fine. That's our agreement," he said, adding that I would hear from him shortly about some other arrangement— not in the FAA, but elsewhere in the Department of Transportation.

Many days later I visited Heffelfinger. "You know, Phil," he said, "something's happening over which I don't have a whole lot of control. You're getting an awful blackballing from officials at the FAA. I've had several real attractive positions lined up that I felt you could handle well and where you would be happy. But when the people involved talked with the people in the FAA you just got a terrible blackballing. As a result, things have cooled off."

Then, about the first week in August, Heffelfinger telephoned me again and said he had just the job. It would be in the Department of Transportation, and I would be working directly for the undersecretary.

The post involved running the U. S. International Transportation Exposition which was scheduled for the spring of 1972 at Dulles International Airport near Washington, and it was a job that excited me. I got together all the relevant documents—papers from the White House, executive orders, background discussions on the matter, legislation that authorized it, the legislative history—and I was set.

Then, several days later, I went to see Heffelfinger again. "Doggone it," he said, "don't you know that just last night Mr. Shaffer persuaded the Secretary [Volpe] to transfer this job from the Secretary's office to Mr. Shaffer's office itself? So, I guess I'm no longer in a position to offer you that job."

I didn't know it at the time, but that job was the last hope that might have kept me in the FAA, because formal charges already were being drawn up against me— and while they didn't say so, the principal reason why FAA management wanted me out was that I was too zealous; I had tried too hard, and trying *that* hard just isn't allowed in the FAA.

CHAPTER XVII

THE CHARGES

I suppose I should have realized what was happening shortly after the discomforting meeting with Bert Harding. It should have been obvious from what he said that the FAA would at least be gathering evidence against me, but I really didn't comprehend the full import of it until nearly a month had passed. Early in July, Archie W. League began to get the wheels into motion.

League and Harding began their search for evidence against me with a very private investigation of all my expense vouchers for the eleven years that I had been an FAA employee. At first the auditors were reluctant to make such an investigation because they weren't simply checking a batch of vouchers from a variety of employees —which normally is their job—but were just looking at one individual's file. As a result, they requested a written order to conduct such a search, which they received from League. The result of this huge search, which must have consumed several days of an auditor's time, considering the sizable amount of traveling I'd done in my time with FAA, was one slightly dubious payment made to me in the amount of $5.25. But we're getting ahead of our story.

The Harding-League case against me began to build up in early July 1970. In rapid succession I received three letters from Archie W. League, that expert bureaucrat who had been put to work to force me out of government. Within five days in early July I received these notices from League:

July 2:

"On 26 June 1970 you mutilated your time and attendance record by removing from it a charge of annual leave for a period of one hour on 16 June 1970 during which you were not present for duty.

"You previously took a similar action to mutilate your time and attendance record for absence of two hours from duty on 19 May 1970, about which I wrote you a letter on 28 May 1970.

"Since our time and attendance clerk is the only person in this office who is permitted to make entries on or to remove data from time and attendance records, and since I am charged with the responsibility of certifying to the accuracy of these records, I request you advise me in writing why you mutilated your time and attendance record and, further, why you should not be charged with annual leave for that period on 16 June 1970 when you were not present for duty."

"Archie W. League."

July 6:

"On Thursday, 2 July 1970, you were charged with 8 hours sick leave. Since only 3 hours sick leave remained to your credit at the time this period of 8 hours of sick leave was taken, your sick leave account is now overdrawn by 5 hours.

"Please submit a request for advanced sick leave in accordance with Agency Order 3600.4, Change 2, dated 2 April 1970, Part 40, subparagraph b., in order that a determination can be made with respect to the granting of advanced sick leave in this instance."

"Archie W. League."

July 7:

"On 2 June 1970 you were assigned Project EV-70-2, subject: 'Survey of Agency Field Evaluation Activities.' [The seven-week trip]

"Since that time you have failed to carry out your responsibilities to administer and to carry out this assignment. You sent to me Mr. Richard A. Harris, GS-15 Evaluation Specialist, to work out the details of administering this project. You have failed to maintain personal contact with me on this project or on any other matters pertaining to the operation of your Division or the Office of Appraisal since this project was assigned.

"You presented to me on 4 June 1970 a letter from Dr. Richard J. Mulvaney stating that you should not be permitted to travel because of certain physical disabilities.

"On 5 June 1970 I advised you that in view of your disability it would not be desirable for you to travel until your health improved. This letter did not excuse you from any of your responsibilities as Chief of the Evaluation Division, yet you have failed to carry out those responsibilities for which you are being paid a salary of $30,972 per annum.

"Please advise me in writing why you have ceased to function as Chief of the Evaluation Division of the Office of Appraisal for the past month so that I may make a proper judgment as to further action in this matter."

"Archie W. League."

An ordinary person reading this would imagine that League and I were halfway across the country from each other and that League was primarily in charge of recording time and attendance. But the fact was, not only were we in the same building but we were in the same office, separated only by a thin partition. And rather than being in charge of time and attendance and other matters properly the responsibility for a GC 5 clerk, Archie League was responsible for supervising an office whose principal responsibility was determining how well the Federal Aviation Administration was regulating aviation safety and helping to protect the lives of hundreds of millions of airplane passengers yearly. Yet, League expended considerable taxpayers' money by using his own time (at $36,500 a year, or about $20 an hour) and that of his secretary to minutely examine every shred of paper available to him in order to build his case against me.

I didn't answer any of League's letters. I suppose I didn't answer them because I didn't like League. It irritated me, too, because it didn't seem appropriate at my age and station in life to become engaged in an exchange of petty charges of this nature. For League's part, his only reason for writing them was that he knew that in order to fire somebody, you've got to have a sheaf of papers an inch thick documenting your case that the individual you want to dismiss is incompetent, untrustworthy and cheating the government.

During the weeks that followed, little happened except for my conversations and visits with Deputy Assistant Secretary Heffelfinger. I suppose for the most part during those weeks I spent my time studying aviation accident statistics. The round-the-world project I was supposed to have directed was instead being accomplished by Richard Harris and William Evans of my staff, but with the grueling itinerary cut about in half.

Then, on the morning of August 18, Bert Harding's secretary called me. "Mr. Harding wants to see you tomorrow," she announced over the telephone.

"Oh? What's the subject?" I asked.

"He just wants to see you."

"Well, that's fine, I'd like to see him, too, but what's the subject. What does he want to talk to me about."

"Well, Mr. Ryther," she said, in that obnoxious manner secretaries for middle-management government functionaries seem to have, "he just wants to see you at 2:30 tomorrow afternoon."

"Well, fine. You tell Mr. Harding to call me," I said, and I hung up.

Harding never did call back, but within a few minutes a memorandum found its way to my desk:

"Subject: Appointment with the Associate Administrator for Manpower.

"To: Mr. Philip I. Ryther

"I have been advised by Mr. Harding, Associate Administrator for Manpower, that he wishes an appointment with you and with me at 2:30 P.M. on Wednesday, 19 August 1970, in his office. Please make arrangements to be present in his office at that time."

It was signed by Archie W. League.

The next afternoon I appeared at the door to Harding's office at 2:30. When I opened the door and walked in, I found two men there: Bert Harding and Archie League. "Hello, Phil," Harding said. "Hello, Bert," I answered. League said nothing to me, and I didn't speak to him. He just sat in a straight-backed chair with his back to a window across from Harding.

Harding bade me have a seat. There was no offer of coffee on this visit as there had been on the last.

"I want to go over with you again the options we are offering you to give you one more opportunity to understand what I said to you a few weeks ago. I have to add that I believe—although I'm not sure—that I can still accommodate you and work out this retirement of yours without all of the harassment and difficulty and pain it all will cause if we have to do it on an involuntary basis," Harding explained.

And he again went over the three alternatives: I could retire because League and I no longer were compatible; my job could be abolished; or I could face charges. When he finished, he leaned back in his swivel chair and asked, "Well, Phil, which will it be?"

"Bert, my answer is the same one I gave you before. I have no interest in any of these approaches to my career," I said.

"All right Phil, if that's the way you want it, Mr.
League has a document for you."

Archie reached into his briefcase and withdrew what
appeared to be a lengthy letter. He handed it to me. I
asked Harding if there was anything else. He answered
that there wasn't, and I left.

Returning to my office, I closed the door, sat down and
thumbed through the eleven-page letter. It was filled
with the most inane complaints against me, and I found
it unbelievable that a mature man of League's position,
the highest grade possible for a career civil servant,
should have spent as many hours and days at the cost of
literally thousands of hard-earned federal tax dollars on
such childishness as this.

The letter read as follows:

Mr. Philip I. Ryther
Chief, Evaluation Division
Office of Appraisal
Federal Aviation Administration
Washington, D.C., 20590

Dear Mr. Ryther:

This is notice that I propose to remove you from your position of Chief, Evaluation Division, GS-301-16, $30,972
per annum, in the Office of Appraisal, Federal Aviation
Administration, Washington, D.C. This action will not
occur earlier than thirty (30) days from the date on
which you receive this notice.

You have failed to demonstrate the administrative and
management ability commensurate with your responsibil-

ities and you have demonstrated a lack of knowledge of the policies, procedures and practices of the Federal Aviation Administration and the Office of Appraisal as set out in the charges and specifications in this letter.

Charge No. 1. Failure to properly plan, develop and execute evaluation projects of FAA activities.

Specification No. 1.

On 5 September 1969 you recommended the elimination of all air traffic staff personnel in the area offices, the reduction of the personnel in the Air Traffic Division staff in each regional office to ten (10) employees, and the reduction in the Air Traffic Division staff at Washington headquarters from its level of approximately three hundred (300) employees to twenty-five (25) employees. When I discussed your recommendations with you on 5 September 1969 you stated that your reason for this recommendation was that "they have too many people and too much coordination." You did not indicate the factual basis on which your conclusions rested nor did you explain how the present responsibilities and functions of the Air Traffic Service in the area, regional and Washington headquarters offices would be carried out with the reduced staffing you recommended.

Your recommendation and conclusion was not based on any study or evaluation of the Air Traffic Service staff functions and operations at the area offices, regional offices or Washington headquarters.

Specification No. 2.

On 5 November 1969 you submitted to me your plan for an evaluation project of the Flight Standards Service process of certifying airmen and aircraft.

On 6 November 1969 I informed you that the Flight
Standards Service evaluation project was to be broadened
to include all programs, activities, functions and responsibilities of the Flight Standards Service, excepting only
the flight inspection and aircraft management programs
of that service. On 20 November 1969 I authorized you in
writing to proceed with an evaluation of the Flight Standards Service which was to include all programs and
activities of that Service excepting only the flight inspection and aircraft management programs of that Service.
This project was designated EV-69-1.

On 4 December 1969 you and I had a meeting in my
office concerning the focus of the Flight Standards Service evaluation project (EV-69-1). At that time I again
informed you that this project was not to be limited to
the certification programs of the Flight Standards Service but was to include all programs and activities of that
Service except the flight inspection and aircraft management programs.

On 8 December 1969 I informed you in writing that
evaluation project Ev-69-1 of the Flight Standards Service was not to be limited to the airmen and aircraft certification programs of that Service.

You did not prepare or develop an evaluation plan
for the Flight Standards Service evaluation project (EV-
69-1). Since you did not prepare or develop an evaluation
for this project it was necessary for me to prepare the
evaluation plan for you on 15 January 1970.

Specification No. 3.

On 6 April 1970 I received your report on project
EV-69-1, Evaluation of Flight Standards Service. This re-

port did not include the international functions of the
Flight Standards Service, training programs for Flight
Standards Service personnel, the mechanical reliability
reports system, the standard procedures for uniform reporting system, problems in aircraft accident investigation and problems in aircraft registration.

On 14 April 1970 I informed you in writing of the deficiencies in your report including the absence of the
work-indicated subjects from your report. The report was
returned to you for additional work with instructions to
include the above-indicated subjects in your report.

On 28 April 1970 you submitted to me a revised report
on project EV-69-1. This revised report did not include a
discussion of the international functions of the Flight
Standards Service personnel or the problems in aircraft
accident investigation.

Subsequent to 28 April 1970 when I was coordinating
your revised report on project EV-69-1 with the Director
of the Flight Standards Service I learned for the first time
that your report did not include actions already planned
or being implemented by the Flight Standards Service
to correct problem areas of which your report was critical.

Specification No. 4.

On 8 April 1970 you recommended an evaluation project covering the airport planning, financing and development activities of the FAA.

In November 1969 you and I discussed the various
areas of FAA activity which would be appropriate subjects for evaluation studies. At that time I advised you
that the airport planning, financing and development ac-

tivities of the FAA would not be an appropriate subject
for an evaluation study since there was then pending before the Congress proposed legislation in the form of an
Airport and Airways Development Act which if enacted
into law would substantially affect the airport planning,
financing and development operations of the FAA.

At the time of your recommendation the Airport and
Airways Development and Revenue Acts had been passed
by the House of Representatives and the Senate in different forms, and on 8 April 1970 this proposed legislation
was pending before a Congressional Committee of Conference.

Charge No. 2. Failure to comply with the standards
and procedures issued by the Federal Aviation Administration.

Specification No. 1.

On 29 December 1969 you were informed in writing
that one of the members of your division, Mr. Leonard
Quiram, was due an Employee Appraisal Record (EAR)
in order to qualify for a within-grade increase with an effective date of 25 January 1969. You were also informed
that the forms provided to you should be returned to
HQ-110 at least fifteen (15) days before the effective
date of 25 January 1970.

On 12 January 1970 an EAR for Mr. Quiram was sent
to me for my signature after it had been completed by
you. Upon reviewing the EAR you had prepared for Mr.
Quiram it was apparent that the key result areas of the
EAR did not match Mr. Quiram's position description as

a systems analyst, as required by FAA Handbook 3430, "Evaluation and Improvement of Employee Performance," paragraphs 12 and 47.

Because the key result areas of the EAR did not match Mr. Quiram's position description it was necessary for me to rewrite the performance key result areas for Mr. Quiram's EAR. Additionally, because the key result areas of the EAR submitted to me by you did not match the position description of Mr. Quiram and due to the fact that you were out of town on official travel it was necessary for me to request that Mr. Quiram's within-grade increase be processed without the necessary documentation of the EAR.

On 14 January 1970 I requested in writing that you complete Mr. Quiram's EAR as rewritten by me to conform to his position description without delay on your return from your trip. After you returned from your trip it was necessary for me to again request in writing on 9 February 1970 that you complete Mr. Quiram's EAR. You did not submit a completed EAR for Mr. Quiram which matched his position description until 2 March 1970, which is approximately thirty-five (35) days after the effective date and approximately fifty (50) days after the date on which the EAR was due.

Specification No. 2.

On 7 April 1970 I first learned that you had led some members of your staff in the Evaluation Division to believe that they would be promoted to higher grades or promoted to positions which became available in the Appraisal Division. I learned of this when a member of the

Appraisal Division staff transferred to the Air Traffic Staff and members of your staff in the Evaluation Division came to my office to inquire about the expectation of their being promoted to the Appraisal Division job since they had been given to understand by you that all such position vacancies would be filled by promotion of members of the staff of the Evaluation Division.

This action by you was in violation of paragraph 42 of FAA Handbook 3330.1A, "Merit Promotion Program," which prohibits the selection of an individual for promotion based on personal favoritism and which also prohibits the making of such promotion commitments.

Your action was also in violation of FAA Handbook 3330.22, "Executive Selection and Inventory System," which establishes the method by which personnel are selected for promotion to the GS-15 level.

This action by you was in derogation of my duty and responsibility as Assistant Administrator for Appraisal in conjunction with the Chief of the Appraisal Division to seek and try to obtain the best possible qualified individual to fill the vacancy in the Appraisal Division.

Specification No. 3.

On 9 April 1970 you submitted to me in writing a memorandum which requested the Chief of the Personnel Operations Division (HQ-100) to conduct what you referred to as "desk audits" in your division.

Apparently you were unaware of the proper procedures or were unwilling or unable to search for and locate the proper procedures to have positions in your division reclassified. On 13 April 1970 I returned your memorandum of 9 April 1970 to you and at that time I pointed out to you in writing that classification appeals are to be prepared in accordance with FAA Handbook 3510.8, "Position Classification," and that Chapter 4 of that handbook specifically applied to classification appeals.

Specification No. 4.

On 19 May 1970 you were not present for duty from about 10 A.M. to about 12:00 P.M. You did not inform anyone where you could be located. On your return to the office you informed your secretary that you were to be charged with two (2) hours of annual leave. Your Time and Attendance Card was marked to indicate that you had taken two (2) hours of annual leave. You initialed that card.

On 20 May 1970 you crossed out both the charge of two (2) hours annual leave and your initials on the Time and Attendance Card. This action by you is in violation of Paragraph 3 of FAA Handbook 2730.2A, "Time and Attendance," which requires that the actual hours of duty each day and all absences from duty are to be accurately recorded for each employee by the designated time and attendance clerk.

Specification No. 5.

On 16 June 1970 you were not present for duty between 8:30 A.M. and 9:30 A.M. The time and attendance clerk marked your time and attendance card to indicate your absence and you were charged with one (1) hour of annual leave.

On 26 June 1970 you crossed out this charge of one (1)

hour annual leave. On 2 July 1970 I requested in writing that you advise me in writing why you should not be charged with annual leave for the time on 16 June 1970 when you were not present for duty. As of the date of this letter you have not so advised me.

Your action is in violation of Paragraph 3 of FAA Handbook 2730.2A, "Time and Attendance," which required that the actual hours of duty each day and all absences from duty are to be accurately recorded for each employee by the designated time and attendance clerk.

Specification No. 6.

On 13 July 1970 you sent to me for review and signature an Employee Appraisal Record (EAR) for Mrs. Ruth Saghatoleslami, your secretary. Upon reviewing this document I discovered that you had not discussed this Employee Appraisal Record with Mrs. Saghatoleslami nor had you discussed with her any proposals for her development as an FAA employee. Your action was in violation of Chapter 4 of FAA Handbook 3430.3, "Evaluation and Improvement of Employee Performance."

Specification No. 7.

On 8 August 1969 you and I were passengers on Eastern Air Lines flight 142 from Atlanta, Georgia, to Dulles International Airport. We arrived at Dulles Airport at approximately 8:00 P.M. We had been served and had consumed a dinner meal while en route to Dulles from Atlanta. You were travelling on official business and were reimbursed for your actual expenses incurred. On the schedule of expenses submitted by you, you claimed an expense of $5.25 for dinner on 8 August 1969. Your action is in violation of Paragraph 754 of FAA Handbook 1055.13, "Travel."

Charge No. 3. Abuse of subordinate employees.

Specification No. 1.

On 30 October 1969, you asked my secretary, Mrs. Irene Lane, about the status of your procurement request for a desk and telephone to be placed in the conference room. Mrs. Lane informed you that she had been instructed not to request the desk and telephone. You then became loud and abusive as you demanded that Mrs. Lane explain to you why your procurement request had been canceled. Your actions caused Mrs. Lane to become upset, and she informed you that she was accustomed to being treated as a lady.

Specification No. 2.

On 12 May 1970 you became loud and abusive in the presence and hearing of other employees of the Office of Appraisal as you accused your secretary, Mrs. Ruth Saghatoleslami, of listening in on your telephone conversation. Your abusive actions caused Mrs. Saghatoleslami to cry and become extremely upset and embarrassed by you before the other employees of the Office of Appraisal.

Charge No. 4. Insubordination.

Specification No. 1.

On 11 February 1970 I asked if you had any personnel who fit into the Ready Reserve categories set out in Agency Order No. 3300.4A, a copy of which order was given you. I informed you that the information was due on or before 15 February 1970. You responded by saying that you did not know the Ready Reserve status of your personnel but would obtain the information after 16 March 1970. You did not provide me with this information.

Specification No. 2.

On 16 March 1970 I inquired of Mr. Leonard Quiram, a member of the staff of the Evaluation Division, when he was going to brief me on the Flight Standards Service evaluation handbook of the Central Region, which briefing I had requested of him some time previously. Mr. Quiram informed me that you had told him to disregard my request. You issued your instructions to Mr. Quiram to disregard my request without coordinating such instructions with me or inquiring of me the reason for my request to Mr. Quiram.

Charge No. 5. Failure to carry out assignments.

Specification No. 1.

Prior to 11 September 1969 you were informed by me that I had selected you as my representative to attend an important briefing to take place on 11 September 1969 at the Pentagon beginning at 9:00 A.M. concerning logistics being given by Commander, Air Force Logistics Command. You failed to attend this meeting which was held on 11 September 1969 as scheduled.

Specification No. 2.

Prior to 18 September 1969 you were informed by me that I had selected you as my representative to attend a meeting to take place at the Shoreham Hotel at 10 A.M. on the morning of 18 September 1969. You failed to attend this meeting which was held on 18 September 1969 as scheduled.

Specification No. 3.

On 11 February 1970 I requested in writing that you provide me with an inventory of the skills of the individual members of your division. On the same day you submitted to me a list which was incomplete in that it did not include all of the skills of the members of your division.

Charge No. 6. Failure to discharge administrative and supervisory responsibility.

Specification No. 1.

On 28 October 1969 you were being consulted by Mr. Robert Faith, Chief, Appraisal Division, Office of Appraisal, concerning proposals to rearrange office space. You reacted to this consultation by demanding in a loud and abusive voice to know why you had not been previously consulted, and caused a general disruption in the Office of Appraisal.

Specification No. 2.

While I was on official travel for the period of 24 March through 3 April 1970, Mr. Robert Faith, Chief, Appraisal Division, whom I had designated to act for me in my absence, requested that you accept a designation of Acting Assistant Administrator for Appraisal for a period of two (2) days while Mr. Faith was on annual leave. You refused to be designated as Acting Assistant Administrator for those two (2) days.

Specification No. 3.

On 9 June 1970 you issued an authorization for a travel advance in the amount of $1,024.05 to Mr. Richard Harris of your staff for forty (40) days of travel. You issued this authorization despite the fact that the trip called for only eighteen (18) days of travel and only twenty-two (22) days remained in the current fiscal year. You had previously been informed that there was a shortage of travel funds.

Specification No. 4.

On 2 June 1970 you were assigned evaluation project EV-70-2, Survey of Agency Field Evaluation Activities. On 4 June 1970 you handed me a letter from Richard J. Mulvaney, M.D. in which letter the doctor stated that you should not travel because of your physical condition. On 5 June 1970 I informed you in writing that in view of your physical condition it would not be necessary for you to travel until your health improved. My letter to you of 5 June 1970 did not relieve you of any of your responsibilities as Chief of the Evaluation Division.

Since 5 June 1970 you have not provided direction and supervision on a daily basis to the staff members of your division. You have not maintained personal contact with me regarding the planning, staffing, problems or progress in relation to project EV-70-2. You have withdrawn yourself from providing direction, guidance and supervision to the members of the staff of the Evaluation Division.

You may answer these charges personally, in writing or both to me. You may submit affidavits in support of your answer. You will have fifteen (15) calendar days from the date you receive this letter to submit your answer. Consideration will be given to extending this fifteen (15) day period in which to answer these charges if you request such an extension from me stating your reasons for desiring more time.

Full consideration will be given to any answer you submit. If you do not understand the reasons for the proposed action contact me for further information.

As soon as possible after your answer is received, or after the expiration of the fifteen (15) days period in which to answer if you do not submit an answer, a written decision will be issued to you.

The letter was signed by Archie W. League. I read the letter, reread it, leaned back and chuckled quietly. There was no doubt that Archie had spent a lot of time on these charges. It was also obvious to me that not one of them could stand up under any scrutiny. I decided it was a power play on the part of League and Harding to scare me, so I decided I wouldn't be scared. But it did accomplish what League and Harding wanted it to accomplish; combined with the disappointing news from Heffelfinger that no job could be found for me anywhere in the Department of Transportation, it made me decide to retire. It seemed that no matter what I said or did, though these charges would never be pursued—they were too ridiculous, and neither League nor Harding would want to stand the embarrassment of having them come out publicly, even before a relatively private Civil Service Commission hearing.

Only two of the fifteen days granted to me to answer

the charges had elapsed before I received another phone call from Bert Harding: would I please stop by his office? Once again, up to the tenth floor, once again through Harding's office door, once again "Hiya Phil, good to see you this morning" from "Bert," and once again Archie League was seated on his same straight-backed chair with his back toward the window. But this time even League said, "Good morning, Phil."

Harding started into his old routine: "Somehow we can work this out, Phil. And we really want to help work this out because it's to your advantage to do it. It's to your advantage to take this early retirement—and that's what we're here for. And frankly, Phil, I've got another idea on this thing. I've prepared another piece of paper here for you to sign and it's addressed to Archie.

"You know Archie's talked about how he wants to reorganize his office and so as a result of the reorganization, your job would be eliminated. And if you request it—now Phil you're going to have to request it—Archie will give consideration to allowing you to retire."

At this point, even Archie joined in the conviviality. "Yes, Phil, if you will sign this letter requesting retirement, we will go ahead with this reorganization, eliminate your job and allow you to retire."

At this, Harding handed me a little piece of paper which bore a note typed by his secretary:

"Archie League

"I understand that you are considering a reorganization of this office and, as a result, may abolish my present job as Chief, Evaluation Division.

"This is to advise that, for personal and health reasons, if your plans mature, or if I otherwise become eligible for a discontinued service annuity, I desire to avail myself of this option.

"I would appreciate your early advice as to whether such an arrangement might be feasible."

The letter was meant to be retyped by my secretary for my signature.

I agreed, but suggested that I be allowed to remain at the FAA until the end of the year, citing the fact that I had heavy expenses for medical care for my daughter, and sizable college costs for my other two children. The 60 percent cut in pay as a result of retirement would put me in a severe financial bind. Harding agreed.

Harding and League devised a complicated plan for the manner in which my retirement would be handled. First, I would write a letter to League such as the draft which he had handed me. League would in turn write a letter requesting my resignation. I would then write a letter of resignation which FAA would use as the basis for recommending to the Civil Service Commission that I be granted a discontinued service annuity (retirement at earlier than the normal age) effective December 31. I would then go to the Civil Service Commission and apply for retirement and obtain that agency's approval for the discontinued service annuity.

Then Harding suggested that at the time I give League my letter of resignation, I should also hand him back his letter of charges on an informal basis. I felt that this would be incriminating. Because the charges had been formally drawn up and presented, it seemed to me that I should either return them to League with a memorandum explaining the entire matter, or that League should write me a letter requesting return of the charges.

"Phil, that just can't be done," Harding said, "but let's just all have the understanding that the letter of charges will have the status of never having been written. And I want to impress upon you, Phil, that it's extremely important that no copies of that letter be made."

Harding said—and League confirmed—that the only copies of the letter were those in League's file. No other copies had been made, and none had been sent to my personnel file.

I returned to my office at 10:30 that morning. Not fifteen minutes later my old friend Heffelfinger called. "Yes, Phil, it will be fine with the department if you want to retire effective December 31," he said. I had to admire this fast communication.

My retirement, however, was not destined to be that easy, for despite League's bureaucratic expertise, he and his friends had made an incredible administrative error.

CHAPTER XVIII

VERDICT: GUILTY OF EMBEZZLING $5.25

Four days after the meeting in Harding's office at which I thought my retirement had been worked out, League popped into my office. We hadn't been on speaking terms for months, but by this time—due no doubt to my pending retirement—we were good friends once again.

I remember that Archie came into my office that August 25 and stood at the corner of my desk. He seemed happy, marvelously happy that everything was working out so well.

But there was one minor detail: "Phil, Bert has sent this paper down and here's a draft of a new letter he says is necessary before we can get your retirement cleared with the Civil Service Commission."

The draft he handed me said: "In response to your request, I hereby submit my resignation effective 31 December 1970. This resignation is made with the understanding that misconduct or delinquency is not involved and that this resignation will entitle me to an immediate discontinued service annuity. My application for retirement is attached."

So they'd finally caught on to their error, I thought. They had decided not to abolish my job after all. Had they gone through with their original plan and abolished my job, I would have been able to step into virtually any job in the FAA which was then being filled by someone with less service and time than I had. Obviously, League and Harding had discovered this loophole and decided I might take the option and remain in the FAA.

That same day—August 25—I received the expected note from League: "On 19 August 1970, we discussed your inability to work harmoniously with your immediate supervisor on policy matters. The results of that discussion led to the conclusion that the only satisfactory solution to that problem is to obtain your resignation.

"You are, therefore, requested to submit your resignation to me effective no later than 31 December 1970."

The following day I had another talk with League, this time about my forthcoming visit to Andrew E. Ruddock, director of the Civil Service Commission's Bureau of Retirement, Insurance and Occupational Health. Ruddock had to clear such an unusual retirement as mine, and needed to meet with me.

League warned me not to reveal to Ruddock that the FAA had placed charges against me but had agreed to withdraw them if I would retire. He said Ruddock had not been told about this little matter by Harding when the two discussed the retirement. Ruddock, League said, had consented to the retirement without knowing about the charges. Ruddock had merely been informed that I was submitting my resignation. League pointed out that the draft of my proposed resignation letter said I was resigning "with the understanding that misconduct or delinquency was not involved" in the matter. He said that wording had been given to him by Bert Harding and had been cleared with Ruddock.

I had met Ruddock only one other time, so I barely knew him when I walked in and shook hands with him the next day. I showed him the draft of my resignation letter and told him I understood it had been cleared by him.

"Yes, yes, this is fine. It's a procedure we have to go through to handle one of these things," Ruddock said.

"Well," I said, "now with respect to this statement in this draft letter about no misconduct or no delinquencies, I just can't sign that."

"Why not?"

"Because it's a false statement," I admitted, because I knew that if I signed the statement and somehow word of the charges against me got out I could not only lose my retirement, but possibly face prosecution.

"A false statement? What do you mean?" Ruddock asked.

I took the eleven pages of charges out of my briefcase and showed them to him.

"Oh, well, well, well. I certainly didn't know about this," he said, "and you tell me now that these are still in effect. We have an entirely different matter here and I certainly can't approve this. You go back to the FAA and they'll be in touch with you."

I left Ruddock's office and returned to the FAA. And, just as he had said, they were indeed in touch with me.

On my return a call was already waiting for me telling me to report to Harding's office.

I rode the elevator to the tenth floor, opened Harding's door and there they were—Bert Harding in his high-backed swivel chair, and Archie League in his straight-backed chair by the window. This time Bert didn't offer me any coffee. In fact, he barely said hello. He was fuming. His normally ruddy face had turned scarlet when I walked in.

"Well, I've had a call from Andy Ruddock," Harding said, glaring at me. "We thought we'd had this all cleared and everything was all set—and we did have it all set so this thing would work out just like you wanted it to.

"But no, you weren't satisfied. Good, old, honest Phil Ryther. You had to go over to the Civil Service Commission and screw the whole thing up.

"Now I can't tell you anything. The only thing I can see now is to force the charges and bring them against you and let the chips fall where they will."

I suggested, "Well, let's go ahead."

Harding's demeanor changed slightly. "I don't have any idea whether I can get this mess straightened out now or not—but I'm going to try. And I can't assure you, Mr. Ryther (no longer Phil), at all that we can now process these papers so it's all set to go. But I'll do what I can."

It was clear to me by this time that Harding had no real intention of pushing the charges against me. Nor was his promise that he would try to "get this mess straightened out" necessarily for my benefit. It was obvious that he had been told by top department officials to get this thing solved. Undoubtedly he found his task a difficult one since the Civil Service Commission had become suspicious of him when I showed Ruddock the charges along with Harding's draft which promised that there were indeed no charges.

The next day, August 28, I drafted my own letter of resignation to Archie League: "In response to your request, I hereby submit my resignation effective 31 December 1970.

"This resignation is made with the understanding by you and by me, and such other Government officials who may be concerned, that misconduct or delinquency is not involved and that this resignation will entitle me to an immediate discontinued service annuity and that I be advised in writing by 2 September 1970 that my resignation has been accepted under the above conditions."

That was Friday. The following Monday, I heard from Archie. His page-and-a-half letter indicated that the FAA had caved in on the Ryther court-martial.

The letter referred to my forthcoming retirement and to my letter of the twenty-eighth of August to League: "Based on discussions with the Civil Service Commission, there is an issue which must be resolved before a determination can be made as to your eligibility for discontinued service annuity. One of the charges and several specifications in my letter to you dated 19 August 1970 might prejudice your eligibility for such retirement. Therefore, it is important to dispose of these issues before accepting your resignation and before sending your application for discontinued service annuity to the Civil Service Commission for decision.

"Charge No. II, Specifications 4, 5, and 7 might be considered to involve misconduct and delinquency. Therefore, I am asking at this time that you reply only to the above Charge and Specifications. After receiving your reply, a determination will be made as to whether these specifications are valid. If the Charge and Specifications are found to be valid, it would appear that you are not eligible for discontinued service annuity. On the other hand, if the Charge and Specifications are found not to be valid, based on your explanation, then it would appear that you would be eligible for discontinued service annuity."

So they had boiled down eleven pages of charges and specifications to maybe half a page of trivia. There were now only three charges: I was absent for two hours from work on May 19, 1970, and changed my time and attendance card from two hours' annual leave to indicate I was at work. (Specification 4.) I was absent from work for one hour on June 16, 1970, and crossed out the notation that charged me with one hour annual leave. (Specification 5.) I had claimed $5.25 for a meal during an official trip on August 8, 1969. (Specification 7.)

My answer to the charges reflected my contempt for the whole silly nonsense. Here's what I wrote to League on September 2, the day after I received his note:

"On May 19th Senator Joseph Tydings, chairman of the Senate District Committee, held hearings concerning the management and operations of National and Dulles Airports. I learned of the hearings after arriving for work that day while you were in the Administrator's daily 8:30 A.M. meeting. Realizing that I had been the leader of the Logistics Service Evaluation Group that had conducted an evaluation of these airports, I felt it proper and important that I be present at the hearings as an observer. Incidentally, many of the findings and recommendations which my group made concerning procurement practices and the collection and accounting for money received from concessionaires at the airports were not acted on by my superiors for almost a year and then they were materially changed. I declined to concur in the action which was finally taken.

"Initially I told my secretary to charge annual leave for the two hours I was in attendance at the hearing. However, after returning to the office I spent additional time conferring with Logistics Service officials and reviewing the evaluation report involved and I, therefore, felt that the entire time should be properly charged as official duty. I requested that my timecard be adjusted accordingly. When I saw my timecard the next day and noticed it had not been adjusted I crossed out the annual leave entry of two hours for May 19. I was told by payroll that to correct an error the entry should be crossed through.

"On June 16, 1970, a five-car accident occurred at the District [of Columbia] end of Theodore Roosevelt Bridge at about 8:15 A.M. I was a few cars back of the accident and was stopped in traffic on the bridge. The overhead traffic helicopter monitored the accident and called for ambulances to remove the injured and tow trucks to remove the vehicles. It was impossible to detour from the accident scene while removal operations were going on. When I arrived for work about 45–50 minutes late I informed one of the secretaries what had happened. I recall working until about 6:00 P.M. that evening on some General Aviation accident reports which had just been received. A week or ten days later I noticed the charge had been made on my timecard for

the 45–50 minutes I had been delayed by the auto accident, so based on the previous advice I received from
payroll I crossed through the entry inasmuch as my being
late was impossible to avoid.

"Perhaps you will recall I left my seat several times
while we were en route from Atlanta, Georgia, to Washington, D.C., on August 8, 1969. I recall mentioning to
you that I did not feel well. It is true we were both
served a meal but perhaps you didn't notice how sparingly
I ate. I'm sure you recall the many times I have told you
of my frequent discomfort as a result of a wartime serv-
ice-connected intestinal disability incurred while serving in the jungle of Burma during World War II. A few
months ago the Veterans Administration found my condition to be aggravated. My family was away from the
city and upon feeling some better I stopped on the way
home from the airport and had a light meal for which I
paid $4.45 plus 18 cents tax, plus 62 cents tip to the
waitress for a total of $5.25.

"Since this event occurred more than a year ago and
you approved my voucher for payment I feel that if you
had a question about the matter it would have been more
appropriate to have discussed it at that time with me.
I believe this to be a proper charge, however, should it
be determined that I'm wrong I'll be glad to reimburse
the government."

My answer did not meet with immediate success.
League told me several days later that all was not well
with the Civil Service Commission. They simply no longer
believed FAA in the matter of my retirement. After having been lied to once, they had no reason to feel that the
FAA was being truthful. Consequently, League wrote me

on September 9 that I would have to answer all of the charges within fifteen days. This, he later said, was simply an attempt to gain more time as he had no intention of prosecuting the remaining charges. He had revealed as much in his September 1 letter.

As soon as I received League's September 9 letter, though, I visited my old friend Heffelfinger, the deputy assistant secretary. "This was all set," I told him, "and then your friends in the FAA screwed it up with the Civil Service Commission by lying to them, and now the Commission won't have anything to do with them, and as a result League has threatened to press all the charges."

"Let me see what I can do about it," Heffelfinger answered, reaching for the telephone. Several days later, September 16, I was called back to Harding's office, but Harding wasn't anywhere to be found. He was working on other matters, now that he was no longer occupied with my case, and the entire matter was being handled by his deputy, E. J. (Andy) Anderson.

"Phil, I've been directed to get this thing solved, and I think I've found a way we can do it. I have here this little letter, and if you'll sign it, I think we'll work things out," Andy told me.

"Another letter," I thought. But it wasn't. Apparently it had been discussed not only within the FAA but with the Civil Service Commission. A few words had simply been jiggled around from my past letters of resignation —otherwise it was the same letter.

In return for signing it, a letter was to be given to me signed by League which, in effect, slapped my wrist for the three minor transgressions. But there was one problem. League, like Harding, had disappeared. "That's OK,

Phil, Bob Faith [League's deputy] can sign it for him," Andy volunteered, and he produced yet another letter, this one signed six days earlier by League saying he was going on a little vacation and in his absence Faith could act for him.

I accepted. League's new letter, dated September 16, was undoubtedly drafted by Anderson. It contained no direct references to obscure FAA regulations, only general statements about them: "Charge 2, Specification 4 pertains to the improper change on your time and attendance card for the charge of two hours annual leave on May 19, 1970. I am not questioning the propriety of your attending a Senate hearing without charge to annual leave; however, such changes must be made by an authorized person who is a time and attendance clerk. Your personally changing the time and attendance card is a technical violation of the FAA system for keeping time and attendance records.

"In Charge 2, Specification 5 the T&A clerk entered one hour of annual leave on your card for June 16, 1970. Your absence on account of a five-car accident, which occurred en route to work is a proper basis for excused absence. Therefore, your explanation is accepted for this excused absence. However, your personally changing the time and attendance card is a technical violation of the FAA system for keeping time and attendance records.

"Charge 2, Specification 7 pertains to your reimbursement of $5.25 for dinner on August 8, 1969. You consumed this meal after your return to your place of duty and, therefore, this is not a permissible reimbursement for your actual expenses of per diem incurred while traveling on official business. Your expense voucher, including the meal, was given administrative approval and subsequently was included in your reimbursement. I am asking the Office of Headquarters Operation to audit this voucher to determine whether this expense should properly be refunded to the Government.

After carefully reviewing Charge 2, Specifications 4, 5 and 7 and your reply, I have determined that there is no evidence to conclude an intent on your part to improperly report your time and attendance, or that you had knowledge that the claim for the meal following arrival at Dulles was not a proper charge for which you should receive reimbursement. Based on this, I am dropping Charge 2, Specifications 4, 5 and 7 of my letter of August 19, 1970. However, you are cautioned that greater care should be exercised in the future in adhering to agency procedures and practices."

Then he made reference to the new resignation letter he had drafted. "Based on your resignation dated September 16, 1970 and your satisfactory response to Charge 2, Specifications 4, 5 and 7, I will not pursue, at this time, the remaining charges and specifications . . . with the understanding that the remaining charges and specifications will be used to pursue your proposed removal from the service should your resignation not become effective on or before December 31, 1970."

My new resignation letter said simply that "I hereby re-submit my resignation effective 31 December 1970. This resignation is based on your request and with the understanding that there is no misconduct or delinquency involved and that this resignation will entitle me to an immediate discontinued service annuity." It was addressed to League.

Several weeks passed during which I had virtually nothing to do. On October 5 League sent me another letter—this time accompanied by a copy of a letter from Andrew E. Ruddock to Andy Anderson. It affirmed my resignation, said it had been "submitted in response to the agency request," and held that it was "involuntary for retirement purposes and independent of charges of misconduct or delinquency." He based his finding on the belief that the "current unresolved charges relate to failure to fulfill the requirements of high standards of service rather than to misconduct or delinquency." As a result, he said, I was at least entitled to retirement pay. But that wasn't my last scrape with the FAA.

CHAPTER XIX

A FRUSTRATING END

Obtaining my retirement apparently wasn't sufficient for League. Now he was determined to see that I didn't even get the proper salary to which I was entitled. Civil Service regulations provide for so-called "within-grade" salary increases. These are much the same as those in many private firms in which an employee's service is reviewed periodically—perhaps once a year or so—and a determination is made whether the employee deserves an increase in compensation because of his increased efficiency or performance. It is not—technically, at least—automatic. For such an increase the government states that the employee must have performed competently, and that he must have conducted himself without disgrace and with good demeanor. In practice such raises are granted almost automatically.

I suppose that in my twenty-six years in government I had received within-grade increases in probably twenty-five years. On September 19, 1970, however, I had completed what amounted to a 104-week waiting period for a within-grade salary increase. At the end of this period, Archie League, my supervisor, determined that I had not performed competently during the previous two years, which, of course, included the time I spent on our big aviation safety evaluation.

Although these increases are not automatic, probably fewer than one in a hundred employees is denied a within-grade raise, and Civil Service Commission regulations require that an employee whose raise is to be denied must be notified on the date the increase is normally due. In my case, however, nothing at all happened—at first.

Not having heard anything, I decided to bring the matter up with League myself. I broached the subject with him toward the end of September. "Phil," League said when I mentioned it, "I would prefer not to answer you, but if you insist I'll give you an answer: it's going to be a denial."

I never insisted on a formal denial of the increase—one of perhaps one thousand dollars a year, and some slight increment in my retirement pay—but I got a formal letter from League rejecting the increase. It was dated September 29, 1970, and, in typical League fashion, it referred to paragraph 31 b (1) of Handbook 3430.3, dated 1 July 1969, which said "if a disciplinary or adverse action based on performance is pending at the time a within-grade increase is due, the increase shall be denied." League pointed out that the charges and specifications in his letter of August 19 were "still in effect but are not being pursued at this time pending your resignation on or before 31 December 1970."

Then he added that I had not been working at an

acceptable level of competence and told me: "Your performance has necessitated the filing of charges against you, constituting a proposal to remove you from your position and, also, is considered sufficient grounds to not recommend the within-grade increase."

Civil Service Commission regulations provide for appealing such a decision, and in this case my appeal had to go to League's boss, Kenneth M. Smith. In my appeal to Smith, I noted that League was basing his decision not to authorize my salary increase on the fact that charges were pending against me. I contended, however, that "the reason for the initiation of charges against me was my insistence upon adherence to aviation safety standards.

"In further support of my competence as a Federal employee, I point to the fact that I have been employed by the Federal Government for a period of 26 years and by this agency for a period of 11 years. During all of this time, my work has been judged competent."

I attached to my letter employee appraisal records for the previous four years which showed that I had indeed been a competent employee. In fact, my most recent report, which was for the period ending September 23, 1968, listed me as exceeding requirements in five out of six specific performance areas.

Smith's reply, which I received in early December, was predictable. He agreed with League. But, as he was required to do, he advised me that I could appeal to the Civil Service Commission Board of Appeals and Review. I did.

It took a long time, and I had almost forgotten about the matter when on July 2, 1971, I received a two-and-

a-half-page decision from the board signed by William
F. Berzak, its chairman.

"It is apparent," Berzak wrote, "from a review of the
September 29, 1970 negative determination that the
agency based its determination and decision to withhold
Mr. Ryther's within-grade salary increase upon the fact
that an adverse action against [him] was pending
within the agency.

"While it is true that certain situations might justify
withholding an employee's within-grade salary increase
because his performance was not at an acceptable level
of competence, and also justify taking some type of formal
disciplinary action, each is a separate action that must
stand or fall on its own merits.

"The Board finds that an adverse action against Mr.
Ryther pending within the agency is not a valid basis
for the agency's September 29, 1970 negative determination and decision to withhold [his] within-grade salary
increase because the determination and decision are not
based upon his performance of the essential requirements
of his position."

Thus I was to receive my full pay increase retroactive
to September 20, 1970, plus whatever additional retirement pay that would mean. I had been vindicated—at
least partly.

It was only three days after I got my original letter
from League turning down my pay increase that I received a two-paragraph letter from him informing me that
while the FAA had agreed to put up with me until the
end of December, League wanted me out of his domain.
I was to be detailed to a desk in some far corner of the

Airport Service to serve out my remaining three months
at FAA.

What incredible irony that on the same day that
letter was being prepared on October 2, an airplane
carrying a load of Wichita State University football
players was already on its fateful trip. Archie League, who
refused to accept a report whose recommendations might
have prevented this very accident, was almost at the
moment of the crash silencing probably the only voice
in the agency that had tried to sound a warning.

I was detailed to Clyde W. Pace, Jr., deputy director
of the Airports Service, that part of the FAA which aids
communities, states and regional agencies in the development of airports.

I arrived at his office on October 5 and walked in.
Clyde and I had known each other for years, and there
was an immediate air of informality. Clyde casually said,
"I really don't care to go into the whys and wherefores of
why you're here, Phil." I agreed, and we settled down
to try to figure out how I could productively spend my
last three months in the FAA.

Clyde had been thinking about the whole question of
environment and ecology, which was being widely discussed. He was faced with how building airports disturbs
communities, ecology and wildlife, and he wanted me to
consider how the Airports Service should approach this
subject.

Clyde went on: "We've got to have studies. We've got
to have reviews in each case. And in all cases these are
made by cities or states or regional airport authorities.
It would help us if you would give us your judgment as

to how we can advise these cities, states and regional
agencies to go about the evaluation of the ecological and
environmental problems facing them in building new or
expanded airports."

That, in effect, is what I did for my remaining days
in FAA. I looked at such history as there was, mainly
legislative history, and spoke with some friends around
the country who were with engineering or management
firms doing this kind of work for local and state govern-
ments. I delivered my findings in two or three oral reports
to engineering groups in the Airports Service.

And before I knew it December had rolled around.
Since I had had some leave coming, although I was
scheduled to retire December 31, I decided that my last
day would be the twenty-third.

My last couple of days were uneventful, spent mainly
in checking out of the agency. And among the offices
through which I passed was the cashier's office where,
on December 21, I paid $5.25, thus putting to rest any
claim Archie League would have that I had embezzled
that amount from the government. My receipt—which
I have retained—notes that the payment was made to
reimburse the FAA for "Overpayment of Travel Voucher."
The note on the collection voucher says: "We have been
advised that the dinner cost for the 8/8/69 which you
claimed on your voucher dated 9/15/69 was procured
in the Washington area after official travel had ended,
therefore you should not have been reimbursed the $5.25."
So much for embezzlement.

Finally, December 23 came. Much of the day was
taken up by old friends who dropped by to chat for a
few minutes and to wish me luck. About mid-afternoon

I rode the elevator down to the executives' garage, climbed into my car and left.

It was indeed an unceremonious and frustrating end to twenty-six years of government service.

CHAPTER XX

THE WHITE HOUSE

In the days following my "retirement" from the FAA I began to brood about the fate of my report. I knew that unless some action were taken to force the FAA to take notice of the results of those months of work and thousands of man-hours of its own staff's time, the report would simply remain packed away in a filing cabinet, destined never to be seen.

At least one friend suggested that one way to bring it to life would be to write a book about what he called my incredible experience. With his help, word was passed to several individuals in Washington's vast news corps. I received indications of interest from Clark Mollenhoff, Pulitzer prize-winning correspondent of the Des Moines *Register and Tribune*. Mollenhoff contacted Gardner Cowles, president of Cowles Communications, Inc., which published, in addition to the *Register and Tribune*, the now-defunct *Look* magazine.

Before long, Mollenhoff had written a lengthy piece

about my problems with the FAA, and Christopher S. Wren, *Look*'s Washington editor, had prepared an article for the *Look* magazine issue of March 9, 1971.

Several days before *Look* magazine's story of my report on aviation safety and my subsequent forced retirement from the FAA was to appear on the newsstands, I was provided with an advance copy of the article. I decided that although the article already was printed and magazines were about to be distributed, it might still be a good idea to notify the White House, since nothing could be done to stop the bad publicity that the Department of Transportation and the FAA would get, the administration might take a position of acting on our report.

I had known for years some people in the Office of Management and Budget, which is a major policy-making organization within the White House complex. Not only does it examine budget requests from agencies, but it examines and passes upon virtually every piece of legislation sent up to Capitol Hill by the administration. So powerful is OMB, that it has been known to halt legislation backed by cabinet members.

My call to OMB was answered by Charles R. Perry, special assistant to OMB Director George P. Shultz (a former Secretary of Labor). I explained to Perry about the advance copy of the *Look* magazine article that I had, and expressed the thought that some representative of the White House staff probably would like to see it before it was distributed. Without any hesitation in his voice he asked me to bring it in the same day, February 19, 1971.

After the inevitable searches and signatures I was

allowed inside. The Executive Office Building, just west of the White House, is practically as secure as the White House itself, thus discouraging visitors—both unexpected ones and those who are expected but whose arrival might embarrass the individual who extended the invitation. On my arrival at Perry's office, I found two of his associates there: Charles F. Parker, assistant to the assistant director of OMB, and Al Fry, a budget examiner for OMB who is in charge of examining FAA appropriations. The three were waiting for me and said little more than "Hello" when I walked in. Immediately I produced the article, and my single copy was sent out to one of the thousands of Xerox machines in the government, where three additional copies were made.

We sat around the big mahogany table in Perry's office —the three of them quietly studying the article for about fifteen minutes. At the end of the reading I thought there would be a series of questions, or at least some desire for elaboration. But there was none. Since nobody asked me any questions, I decided to ask them one: "Well, gentlemen, what are you going to do with this?"

Perry volunteered an answer: "Within the hour we will have this over to the President's office." Naturally, I didn't think he meant the President himself would see it—few people in Washington ever do when they say that something is being examined by the "President's office." They usually mean someone in that close group that surrounds the chief executive, in this case perhaps John Ehrlichman, Harry Dent, H. R. (Bob) Haldemann, or Peter Flanigan. After Parker gave me his answer there was another period of silence. I took that to mean that my presence no longer was desired. So I left.

About a week later I phoned Perry to ask what had happened. "Gosh, I just don't know," he answered, "we sent it to the President's office and we've heard no more about it."

For that matter, neither have I ever heard any more about it from Perry's office.

That, however, was only my first brush with the White House.

CHAPTER XXI

THE SENATOR

Shortly before the *Look* article appeared, Mollenhoff had taken a draft to Senator James B. Pearson, Republican senior senator from Kansas, who naturally had been intensely interested in the accident that killed members of the Wichita State University football team and in the events surrounding it.

Mollenhoff, I felt, had laid excellent groundwork for me to visit Pearson, who was ranking minority member of the Aviation Subcommittee of the Senate Commerce Committee. It is this subcommittee that exercises so-called "oversight" functions over the FAA—meaning it is supposed to make certain FAA is carrying out the laws that Congress has passed concerning the agency. Further, the subcommittee is interested in a wide variety of aviation matters. If anybody would be interested in how the FAA brushes off safety problems, I reasoned, it would be Pearson.

My first contact with Pearson's office was a telephone

call I made in mid-February 1971 to Robert Woody, an assistant to Pearson. "Yes," he said, he was indeed present when Mollenhoff showed the advance copy of the *Look* article to the senator. "I would very much like to discuss the matter with you myself," Woody told me. "Can you drop by?"

A day or two later I was in Woody's office. The entire matter was outlined in the *Look* magazine article, which was essentially the story of our safety report and the manner in which the FAA treated it, and the FAA's decision to force me out of the government. The story, Woody said, was a "distasteful . . . terrible thing. The senator has read it and it has him extremely disturbed." As a matter of fact, Woody added, "the senator was so exercised about this because the community which had been so upset had just begun to settle down and return to living somewhat of a normal life after this terriblo disaster had happened to those young people. And now, here, this article is going to break the whole thing wide open again. The community wants to forget this thing; they want to put it to rest, and now it's going to be stirred up again."

I told Woody I thought I understood how the people felt and how the article would cause such problems, but that certainly was not the intent of the article. "The intent," I told him, "was that the country ought to get some insight as to the background of what went on and know just how their FAA really treats air safety." Woody then suggested that it might be a good idea for me to discuss the matter with Senator Pearson. The senator was "away from the city back in the state," Woody said, but he would return in a few days.

We spent several minutes discussing our group of evaluators in the FAA, how we had prepared our report, and what we had found. I didn't ask Woody to take any action, although I recalled having read earlier in *Aviation Daily*, an authoritative trade journal of the aviation industry, that Pearson had announced the Aviation Subcommittee would hold hearings on the Wichita State accident—an announcement later expanded to include the Marshall University accident in West Virginia. Woody brought up the matter himself, and mentioned the possibility of my serving as a witness to explain how the FAA had treated our report on aviation safety and our feeling that the crashes would have been avoided had the agency acted in time.

But he reminded me that Senator Pearson, being a Republican and in the minority in the Ninety-second Congress, did not run the committee. The chairman was Senator Howard W. Cannon of Nevada, a Democrat, who had long been considered a friend of the aviation community, which included the FAA. Woody suggested that it might be a good idea to discuss the hearings with the chief professional staff member of the committee, Robert Ginther.

Senators are very busy people, and with literally hundreds of pieces of legislation passing through the Senate every session, it is not possible for a senator to be thoroughly familiar with each one. Generally, senators become thoroughly conversant with the major issues—the issues by which they stand or fall at elections every six years. Then, each senator usually becomes a specialist in fields that interest him. Generally, these are issues that are under continuing consideration by the subcommittees or committees of which he is a member. But even within a subcommittee, each senator doesn't become an expert on every piece of legislation it handles.

In order to keep themselves abreast of this mass of material, each senator has a number of administrative and legislative aides, or staff members. Each committee and subcommittee, too, has its staff members, whose job it is to lay the groundwork for committee investigations. It is they who actually do the investigating, arrange for witnesses to appear at hearings and ordinarily draft the questions that are asked—whether by committee counsel or by the senators themselves. It is the staff members of both the senators and committees who study the massive amounts of testimony and other material and digest it for "their" senators. It is these staff members, too, who frequently draft legislation, often with outside advice, and frequently with the advice of lobbyists from special interest groups.

Although it is the senators who carefully discuss each piece of legislation in committee "markup" sessions and vote on it, the members of a senator's staff and the members of the staffs of key committees emerge as powerful behind-the-scenes individuals on Capitol Hill. They are much sought after by lobbyists who want to influence legislation, by newspaper reporters and broadcasters, and by anybody else who wants to know what is really happening in Congress.

A good staff member, therefore, has the power to do an immense amount of good for "his" senator. If he knows how to handle the press—which reporters for which newspapers are interested in particular issues—he can obtain a great deal of publicity. If he writes well and is a good investigator, the reports he draws up in the name of the committee and its members will receive wide public exposure. Thus Senate staff work—good or bad—ultimately reflects on the individual senator, his committee or himself as chairman of a committee or a subcommittee.

Realizing the importance of committee professional staff members—and heeding Woody's advice—I decided to call Robert Ginther, the chief professional staff member of the Aviation Subcommittee, around the end of February. I made an appointment and about March 1 saw Ginther.

He had, he said, read the *Look* magazine article and, "just wanted to see what the fellow looked like who caused all that trouble over at the FAA."

Then, after a bit more light discussion, he said he would very much like to have me help with the hearings. He asked me to prepare a list of witnesses, the order in which they should be called and a set of questions. I told him "I'd be glad to cooperate," but I needed my old files in the FAA, particularly the several hundred interviews of government employees, industry representatives and others that were collected in the course of our investigation. The FAA had denied me access to these documents previously. And I told him I wanted to work at home.

"We'll get the files, and it's perfectly all right for you to work at home," Ginther declared. "Just take them and work at them when you can. And would you be willing to be a witness and testify before the committee?"

I told him I would be happy to. I left with Ginther saying he would request the FAA to provide their files.

A day later Ginther phoned me and told me he had telephoned the FAA and had told them that he wanted all of the files delivered to the committee. That was indeed good news, I thought.

But then a day or so later, Ginther called me again. This time the news wasn't so good. Kenneth Smith, the deputy administrator, had personally delivered the files to Ginther. But he said he was willing to turn them over to the committee with one understanding; Philip Ryther should not be permitted to see them. Ginther told me that he had acquiesced to Smith's conditions.

"You agreed to let me have the files," I told Ginther. "What do you propose that I do with respect to my commitment to help draft the questions and list your witnesses?"

"Well, the committee is going to have an executive session [a closed meeting] this afternoon and just hold on to everything until you hear from me," Ginther answered.

A day later Ginther was on the phone again. The whole picture had changed, he told me. The approach the committee was going to take would be very different from what we discussed, and it would no longer be necessary for me to draft lists of witnesses and questions. And as far as my being a witness, he would let me know. The committee had decided to call Secretary of Transportation John A. Volpe on the first day and FAA Administrator John Shaffer on the second day. At the conclusion of those two days of hearings, Ginther told me, the committee would determine whether it wished to carry the investigation any further.

Was I to understand that I was or was not to be called as a witness, I asked Ginther. "I can't tell you right now," he answered. It should have been obvious to me at the time that the committee had no intention of calling me or of really getting to the bottom of the FAA's lax handling of aviation safety. It had no intention of ruffling the feathers of the aviation establishment.

The two days of hearings—March 9 and March 10, 1971 —came and went. Volpe never showed up—obviously the hearings were not of sufficient importance to warrant the presence of the Secretary of Transportation. Instead, he sent Admiral Willard Smith, the retired Coast Guard commandant, who had later served as an assistant secretary of transportation in charge of safety and consumer matters. Not even Shaffer appeared. He sent his deputy, Kenneth Smith.

Naturally, with witnesses like that the FAA emerged without a scratch. Nothing new was unearthed. Virtually no attempt was made to find out how the FAA *really* treats aviation safety matters when the results might prove embarrassing to the agency. Senator Pearson asked one question of Admiral Smith about whether he had seen the so-called Ryther report. The old admiral said he had not. Pearson never followed up the question.

I never heard from Ginther about whether further hearings would examine aviation safety any deeper than the superficial one of March. As the days passed without any word, I decided to call him.

Ginther informed me that the committee had concluded that if Senator Pearson—the senator from the home state of Wichita State University—chose to carry the matter any further, the committee would consider more hearings. But otherwise the committee had decided against looking at the matter any further.

Naturally, that was a big disappointment for me. I had hoped that here, at last, all of those months of hard work

by my old FAA staff and me would get a full airing, and
even hoped that we'd be able to push the FAA to take
some positive action to prevent any more of these terrible
tragedies. I decided that if all that was necessary to get
the hearings moving again was a word from Senator
Pearson, I'd try that route. I called Bob Woody in Pearson's office.

"You know, Phil," he said, "we are after all the minority
party. We're not the people who control these hearings.
The chairman has given us no indication he's going to
reconvene these hearings."

That was all I had to hear. It appeared that as far as
Capitol Hill was concerned the matter was dead. The
subject was simply being batted back and forth until I
got the message.

Shortly thereafter, however, Woody telephoned me. He
had made an appointment for me to see Senator Pearson
at 2:30 P.M. on March 16.

"Well, that's fine," I told him, "but what are we going
to meet about?"

"Phil, the senator feels very strongly that you have the
right—and you should be given the opportunity—to express what you've got to say about this," Woody answered.

"Well, I think that's fine, but why can't I be given the
opportunity to express it in a Senate hearing and not in a
conversation?"

"Well, the senator feels very keenly about this and as
a matter of fact he's very disturbed because he under-
stands you're writing a book about it."

"Yes, I am writing a book about it," I answered, both

surprised that he knew about it and miffed at the implication of his statement.

"Well, the senator feels very strongly about your writing a book and making money over a thing like this," Woody added.

"I guess in this country everyone has a right to his own feelings about this matter, but I feel—and you can tell the senator for me—as far as I can see this is none of his business. It's a private matter that I am undertaking on my own," I said, speaking forcefully.

"Well, I've made the appointment for you anyway to see the senator at 2:30 P.M. on Tuesday the sixteenth," he countered.

"Is this a command, an invitation or what?" I asked.

"Phil, let's just say the senator feels that you should be given the opportunity to express how you feel about this whole matter," Woody answered.

"On that basis you can just have the senator call me and I'll be glad to talk with him," I said, somewhat more annoyed than I ought to have sounded.

A couple of days passed; naturally I didn't hear from Pearson. I thought the matter over and concluded that perhaps I ought to have a conversation with him. I called Woody and told him I'd accept the offer he had made for me to see the senator. We made an appointment for March 17, late in the afternoon.

Pearson's office is in the New Senate Office Building, a plain—almost sterile—granite and marble structure northeast of the Capitol. The inside of the building is also plain, and the individual offices aren't much better—all very unimpressive considering the fact that the occupants are among the nation's most powerful people.

I was ushered into Pearson's office at the appointed hour. Only the senator was in the room. He stood up, shook hands, and motioned me toward a chair. One strange sight hit my eyes: his desk was devoid of everything save one piece of paper squarely in the center. It appeared to be a carbon copy of something. I didn't pay too much attention to it, but it was to come up later.

I told Pearson the story of my involvement with aviation safety, my relations with the FAA, and what had happened to me.

"I understand you're going to write a book—or are writing one," the senator said as soon as I had finished.

"Yes, I am."

"You know, I've been asked to write a book several times. And each time I've taken a stab at it and I never seem to get it finished. There just isn't enough time, and I suppose that's one of the penalties of being a senator—you're just so busy, and so pressed with appointments and meetings and the telephone, the letters, that you just never have time to sit and meditate about the bigger things and find a way to express yourself about the big things that are really in front of you. It's a difficult job, writing a book. I've tried it twice and not finished anything. I wish you good luck—you've got a tough proposition ahead of you.

"You know, Mr. Ryther, I'm an aviator myself. I was in the naval air during World War II and flew a great deal, so I have a real practical personal insight into flying in this nation. It's just a stunning thing when we have these terrible tragedies.

"This is certainly also some story that you've told—one I just hated to hear. It's indeed disturbing the things that have happened to you—to a man who tried as you tried. Tell me, why, in your opinion didn't FAA get busy and do something about these things or find that what you had to say wasn't worthy of doing and reject them outright? Is it because they don't have enough people?"

"Senator," I answered, "that is not the reason. FAA has, if anything, too many people."

"Too many people?" he asked, with a surprised expression. After all, he was used to hearing FAA officials excuse their lack of activity on the grounds they simply didn't have the personnel to accomplish all the tasks that Congress had set out for them.

"That's correct," I added, recalling a 1969 recommendation I had made which would have reduced sharply the number of area, region and headquarters staff positions.

"Well, I guess I can understand what you say. I'm always being told that things can't be done because organizations in government haven't enough people. And I always tell them that when you show me that you're getting greater productivity then I'll be glad to show you that yes, you need more people.

"It just seems to me that we're piling people on top of people, and I'm glad to hear you report that, because I've always had the feeling that that is a crutch that the departments fall back on—namely that the Congress hasn't provided them with enough resources. Have we provided them enough? Has the Congress short-changed the FAA? Have we given them enough money? Have we given them enough people?" he asked.

"In my judgment you have," I answered.

Pearson finally got around to the business at hand—the

hearings on the Wichita State and Marshall University crashes: "Mr. Ryther, as you know I have a very keen personal interest in this matter because this happened to friends and relatives of friends in my state. It's a very, very deep matter with me. But with your long government service, I'm sure you know how things work in government and here in the Congress. We have a majority party and a minority party, and I'm a member of the minority party this session. I have never intended and do not intend now to be searching for a scapegoat in this matter. I had been hopeful that the hearings could have been more productive. I don't know whether they will turn out to have been of value or not—I guess only time will give us an answer to that."

Then, turning toward that single sheet of paper on his otherwise empty desk, Pearson said: "This piece of paper, this one here in front of me. I can't show it to you. I will read one part of it to you if I have your word that you will keep it in confidence."

I gave my word. The paper was a letter he had written to Secretary of Transportation John A. Volpe. He said he had met with Volpe and had "understandings" with him concerning the steps Volpe had agreed to take to correct many of the problems of aviation. The letter, he said, was a confirmation of the understanding between the two of them.

"I cannot show it to you," he said, nodding at the letter, "because it's a privileged matter between me and the Secretary. But I want you to know that there has been some attention given to this and that the Secretary feels very keenly about it. The Secretary has indicated some things he intends to do."

Then, before I could probe a bit deeper, Pearson looked at his watch—the obvious signal that the interview was being concluded. "I can't go any further than that—and I see by my watch that we're going to have a roll call in about five minutes. This has been a very interesting visit. I'm certainly glad to have met you. I'm just happy to know that we have people like you in our government, or who were in our government, but I am going to have to leave here in a minute or two."

Before he headed for the door, I asked, "When am I going to hear—and from whom—as to whether anything's going to be done about the things I have told you?" referring to our evaluation of the FAA's lack of activity in aviation safety. "Will I hear, or will the country hear something from the committee? Will I hear or will the country hear something from Secretary Volpe?" I asked.

"Well, I can't tell you about that. I just don't know. You'll just have to wait and see. I'm going to have to run now," Pearson said, and with that he got up and left his office. My interview was over.

I had to put a few things into a briefcase, so I was several seconds behind Pearson leaving his office. Then an odd thing happened.

As I walked out of his office, I saw him striding down the long, marble corridor about thirty feet ahead of me. About halfway down the corridor he stopped and turned around. He noticed I was still there—walking thirty or forty feet behind him. He then turned quickly away from me and kept walking—not stopping or slowing down so I could catch up with him.

I wondered what interpretation to put on that little motion. Here, after all, were two men who had spent an hour or so together—both walking in the same direction, but one far ahead of the other. Why? Had I perhaps made him uncomfortable? Did he simply have to rush off for a roll call? I'll probably never know.

CHAPTER XXII

REPUBLICAN POWER STRUCTURE

It was obvious that neither the Senate Commerce Committee as a group, nor Senator Pearson as an individual, was going to do much about aviation safety. It was equally obvious that the appropriate executive department of the government—the Department of Transportation and its Federal Aviation Administration—wasn't going to do much either. But there was another senator from Kansas who occupied a place somewhere between the executive and legislative branches of government—Robert J. Dole, chairman of the Republican National Committee.

I've always felt that people in government are more likely to become concerned and act on matters if there's a political flavor to them. And since Dole is both a senator from Kansas—where the Wichita State accident was felt most sharply—and was also serving as GOP National Committee chairman, and I was a lifelong Republican, I decided to call his office to discuss with him the possible repercussions that might spring from government inaction in aviation safety.

The phone was answered by Ab Herman, who is just about as folksy as his name would make him sound. He invited me to come over, and when I got to GOP national headquarters, which is in a small building on Capitol Hill just south of the Capitol complex, I gave Herman a brief sketch of what had happened.

"Well, Phil, what do you want us to do? Really, if you were sitting in the chairman's [Dole's] chair what specific action would you take. After all, we're not part of the government, and yet I can understand that this is a matter an office like ours can very well be concerned about. But if you were in his place, what would you do?"

"Ab, if I were in that position I would write a letter to the President saying this matter had been brought to my attention, and that I thought it was a matter of urgency, and that appropriate action should be taken to get to the bottom of it—to find out why the FAA had ignored any number of recommendations made months ago that might have prevented that Wichita State accident."

Herman agreed that that sounded like a good idea. And, of course, he knew Dole was concerned because the accident had been keenly felt by his Kansas constituents. "I'm going to tell him about it, Phil, and I want you to come in and see him. I want you to tell the chairman the story you've just told me. Will you do it?"

I answered that I surely would. Herman added that the chairman "is a very busy man, but I'll arrange it just as soon as I can."

I didn't hear from Ab for a week. So I telephoned him about April 28, about that appointment with Dole. Ab answered: "The chairman's a very busy man; he has many things on his mind; he has hundreds of letters here, all kinds of meetings, traveling around the country. I just haven't been able to arrange it yet."

I reminded Ab that a week had passed. "Yes, I realize that, I realize that. I'll say this, though, I have written a letter from the chairman to the White House on the subject—he still would like to see you—but we have written the White House."

Now, the White House is a very big place, because it includes the Executive Office Building where hundreds of government workers associated with the White House staff work. And letters to "the White House" seldom reach the President himself. So I asked Ab, "Who's the White House?"

"We don't divulge who we write to. When we write to the White House, we write to the White House."

I suggested that maybe he had written to Harry Dent, one of Nixon's many aides. "Well, it might be, but we wrote to the White House. You know the chairman would still like to see you, and I'd still like to get you two together."

That was the last I heard from Ab Herman, though I waited and waited. Finally on the first day of May, figuring that Ab had indeed written to Harry Dent, I called Dent's office to see if I could get somebody—anybody—moving to improve aviation safety. His secretary answered the phone and gave me the usual White House "Mr. So-and-so is very busy right now, but if you can give me some indication of the subject, perhaps I can find somebody else who can help you." I told Dent's secretary the matter had to do with aviation accidents and the Federal Aviation Administration, and my call was referred to Peter Millspaugh, an assistant to Dent.

I told Millspaugh by way of introduction that being a member of the Republican party, I was interested in the quality of our government. I said I felt I could understand quite well the President's occasional chagrin over how some of his subordinates had taken care of matters, and that I didn't want the President to be embarrassed about the problems in his Department of Transportation resulting from the poor management of the FAA. Further, I had understood that the chairman of the Republican National Committee had written the White House a letter on the subject.

"Mr. Ryther, it's always good to talk with somebody on the same wavelength as yourself," Millspaugh said, "especially with somebody who seems to be intrested in improving the government. But can you tell me a little more specifically what the subject is and what you want us to do."

Again I described the familiar story of our report, its relationship to the Wichita State crash and the resulting grief I had suffered at FAA because I tried to go outside normal channels to get some kind of action on the report's recommendations. I reminded him also of the President's expression of sorrow at the time of the Wichita crash for the families who had lost sons, and Nixon's announcement that he was donating from his personal funds to a collection being taken up for the families.

"Yes, Mr. Ryther, there's no doubt it's a very serious subject, and I do remember the attention it got at the time, and I remember well the President's expressions of just what horrible national catastrophes both the Wichita and Marshall University crashes were.

"And I might add that I'm particularly shocked at the treatment you received at the FAA. Let me do this—give me a day or so to look into the matter and I'll call you before twenty-four hours have passed."

Fifteen hours later—at 9 A.M. the following day—a man who identified himself as Barry M. Locke called. Locke was a special assistant to Secretary of Transportation John A. Volpe. Locke introduced himself, saying that the Secretary's office had had a call from the White House—he didn't say who at the White House—and they were concerned because they'd understood that I was writing a book about my experiences and the condition of aviation safety regulation at the FAA. He wanted to know whether this was true. (Apparently I had told Millspaugh that I was preparing a book.) It is interesting that Locke's first thought was not about improving aviation safety, or ironing out the obvious management problems at the FAA, but about the book that I was writing and the publicity it might receive.

Yes, I told Locke, I was indeed writing a book.

"I'm sure glad to talk with you," Locke said, "and I want to assure you that we want to be most helpful. And the White House [again he didn't say who] is most anxious that we get into this with you. Could you tell me, Phil, what the thrust of your book is?"

By this time I'd become annoyed that he was being somewhat presumptuous, so I gave him a circular answer, telling him it was "about the conditions of things."

"I'm sorry, Phil, but I don't understand you. What

I want to know is what the thrust of the book is going to be."

"Well, it's about conditions we found—conditions."

"Phil, I don't think we're communicating."

"Well, I don't know whether we are or not, because I have no idea why you've called me."

"I'm calling you because the White House has called us asking us to be helpful."

"That's very generous of you to offer your help," I said.

"Phil, could you come in and discuss it?"

"Well, I'm pleased with the invitation."

"Great, how soon can you come in?"

"Well, I've no need to come in now, I'm really doing fine, but as soon as the need arises I will let you know."

"Phil, I still don't think we're communicating. Do you feel we are?"

"I really don't know, because I still have no idea what you're calling me for."

"Well, Phil, could you come in and talk with the Secretary?"

"I'd be tickled to death to talk to the Secretary, and I'm really happy that such an invitation is mine."

"Wonderful, when would you like to come in?"

"I really don't need to come in now, because I have no need to talk with the Secretary. But when something does come up and I need to, well, I will be right on the phone and pick up the invitation."

"Phil, it's obvious we're not communicating—we just don't seem to be getting anyplace."

"Frankly," I said, finally deciding to stop circling around, "I really have no idea what we're talking about or why you've called, inasmuch as it was Mr. Millspaugh at the White House with whom I spoke, and he said he was going to look into the matter and call me within twenty-four hours. And frankly I don't much like the idea of being brushed off this way."

With that, the conversation ended.

I had, of course, wanted Millspaugh to bring the subject to the attention of somebody at the White House who would get to the bottom of what amounted to serious dereliction of administration of safety regulations at the FAA, and force the Department of Transportation to take some action.

It was apparent to me that Millspaugh had thought I simply wanted my old job back—or wanted something for myself from the government—so he or his office called Barry Locke, in the Department of Transportation.

I did not feel that turning the matter over to some special assistant in DOT who really had no knowledge of the subject—and who was obviously giving me the idiot treatment—was in any way a solution to the problem that lay before the nation: how to make aviation safer.

When I finished with Locke, I tried to telephone Millspaugh. His secretary first said, "Just a moment," which was a good indication that Millspaugh was present. But when she returned to the phone, she told me he was busy and would not be able to talk with me.

I asked her to tell Millspaugh that I had called and would like to have him return my call, and that I did not intend to call him again.

He never did. Nor did I.

CHAPTER XXIII

THE SAFETY BOARD

Having tried unsuccessfully to force some kind of action by appealing to a senator whose constituency was intimately involved in the Wichita crash, the chairman of the Republican National Committee and the White House staff, I decided that perhaps an approach to the National Transportation Safety Board might be useful.

I decided to approach the board not only because it had investigated both the Wichita and Marshall University crashes, but also because of its reputation. In four years since its creation as a virtually independent agency (although it is part of the Department of Transportation for administrative purposes) the board had gained a reputation for being a tough, impartial outfit. In its efforts to make transportation safer it had criticized—presumably without hesitation—even its sister agency, the FAA.

The NTSB in 1967 took over the old Civil Aeronautics Board Bureau of Safety, as well as federal safety responsibilities for railroads, buses, seagoing transportation and pipelines. Its approach is to investigate major transportation disasters not only looking for their immediate causes, but seeking action that could be taken to prevent similar incidents in the future.

In the course of its investigations, the board often holds public hearings. Generally it limits participation in these hearings to those who can prove they have some technical expertise in the matter under consideration. In this sense, therefore, while the hearings are held in public, the board has attempted to exclude individual members of the public from giving their views, even if they were intimately connected with the accident under investigation.

Once the NTSB completes its investigations and makes its findings, it can only recommend action that can be taken to prevent future accidents. It has no power to enforce its recommendations. In fact, several of its five board members have opposed any move to give it this power since having to force an agency to accept a recommendation would publicly show it had not already implemented the recommendation, as it should have, and embarrass the agency. As things stand, an agency like the FAA may say it is following an NTSB recommendation, but may implement the change as slowly as it pleases. The FAA may say that the reason for its lack of speed in setting up a new regulation is that its administrative procedures are inherently slow. While this may be one reason for the FAA taking its time, another is to give the aviation industry and the airlines time to adjust to the economics of any new rules.

Anyway, knowing that the NTSB has at least a reputation for making public virtually any reports it makes or receives, and any actions it takes, I decided to appeal to it. I hoped that this agency would pry loose from the FAA our set of recommendations on aviation safety and make them public, allowing the people to judge for themselves whether the FAA was really failing in its regulation of aviation safety. I had known that the safety board had been dealing with the probable cause of the Wichita State and Marshall University accidents for many months, and—especially in view of the *Look* magazine article and the general chattiness of the Washington aviation community—I had hoped that the board might seek me out. Although our report was never made public by the FAA, the fact of its existence was known to hundreds of individuals in the FAA and in the general aviation community.

In early June 1971 I decided to telephone the safety board, and I was referred to the senior member of the board who had been in charge of investigating the Wichita State disaster—retired Coast Guard Rear Admiral Louis M. Thayer. The admiral was well acquainted with me, at least by reputation. "Oh, yes, you are the Mr. Ryther about whom the *Look* article was written. I've talked with some of the staff on the board and they know of you from having worked in the FAA," he said after I introduced myself.

I asked Thayer whether he had seen my report. He had not. I asked further, since it had been many weeks since the *Look* magazine article had appeared, whether the FAA had offered the report, or whether the board had called for it. Thayer said the FAA indeed had not offered it, but he didn't know whether anyone connected with the NTSB had sought it from the FAA—although he knew that it had not been given out for general distribution within the board.

Thayer then volunteered that the board had received new evidence in connection with the Marshall accident and the investigation would be reopened for several additional days of hearings in late June. He suggested I attend the hearings.

The conversation ended about there, but I decided several days later to call him again. Had the board decided to reopen the Wichita hearings, I ventured? "No, I have no knowledge that would lead me to believe we are going to reopen it," he said, "but you never know. If some new information comes to light—as it has in the Marshall University case—it is subject to reopening."

Then Thayer volunteered that shortly after our last telephone conversation he had mentioned our talk and the subject of our aviation safety report at a board meeting, "and it was the consensus of the board membership that you should be invited in for a discussion with the members. I guess I haven't followed through on this as I should have, because the board would like to meet with you." I answered that I would be happy to meet with the board, and we set the date for the next day—June 4, 1971—at 10 A.M.

The board's offices are located on the eighth floor of 800 Independence Avenue, Southwest, the same white granite building that houses my old home, the FAA. I arrived at Admiral Thayer's office at the appointed time. In typical Coast Guard fashion, the admiral offered me a cup of coffee, and for about five minutes we chatted informally. Then he noted that the other board members were waiting and he called them in.

The NTSB is a five-member board, but two members were then out of town—Chairman John H. Reed, a Republican and a former governor of Maine who had served on a presidential highway safety committee, and Isabel A. Burgess, a former Arizona state senator who had an active interest in both highway and aviation safety. Present for the meeting were Acting Chairman Francis H. McAdams, the only member of the present board with past aviation experience, a former member of the Civil Aeronatics Board, a pilot and a lawyer with a background in aviation accident investigation and litigation; Oscar M. Laurel, a Texas lawyer and former state legislator whose only connection with aviation was as a teacher of bomber mechanics during World War II; and Thayer, who brought to the board his expertise in maritime safety matters acquired through a long career in the Coast Guard.

Thayer opened the meeting by introducing me to the members and pointing out that McAdams was acting chairman that day. He reminded the members of our previous telephone conversations, and the fact I had been invited in to discuss the report and my background.

I began by asking what were the ground rules—was the session being recorded? No, it was not, they answered —it was simply a free-wheeling discussion among four men.

I suppose I spoke for eight or ten minutes. I covered the background of my evaluation group, the history of our being assigned as evaluators by the deputy administrator, the methodology we used in conducting our evaluations and the writing of our report. I did not discuss the contents of the report—but only why and how we had prepared it. I had a reason for withholding the essential information of what was in it, which was soon to become apparent. I discussed also the fact that the report had not been properly forwarded and had been delayed along the line for many months. I described my attempts to bring the matter to the attention of Deputy Administrator Kenneth Smith and to Administrator John Shaffer, and the only result of these attempts—my being reprimanded for going outside normal channels. I described the letters I had written to Undersecretary James M. Beggs, and I concluded by saying that I felt that the report contained material that could have a direct bearing on the Wichita and Marshall University accidents.

"Gentlemen, this in effect is the background of how our FAA has handled the safety problem. And I tell you that this report contained specific recommendations that are directly related to the Wichita accident. And since you are not privy to this report, I thought you would want to know about it."

A few seconds of silence greeted the conclusion of my statement. Then board member McAdams looked up at me. His face appeared flushed, although this was neither the flush of anger nor frustration but a permanent flush: "Well, Mr. Ryther, now that we've heard your life story, how do you propose to save all these people's lives. If you don't have a proposal of how to save lives, I don't see what you're talking about except to try to tell us the tale of your life."

I was shocked and confused at such an unexpected

attack. "Are you the acting chairman of this board today?" I asked.

"I am," McAdams shot back.

"Well, I guess that from such a question I understand the extent of concern and interest that you people have for this matter. Unless somebody has some more questions, why I'll leave," I said, looking around at all three.

Thayer interrupted. "Oh, no, no. Please stay, I think we want to discuss this thing some more," he said, in an obvious attempt to play down McAdams's outburst.

"Admiral," I said, "this question that has just been posed to me is insulting and I just don't see that there's any point in my staying on any more."

At this point McAdams came back in: "Well, Mr. Ryther, you talk about one hundred seventy lives, two hundred lives—"

"Fifteen hundred lives now," I put in.

"Well, all right, you say it's fifteen hundred lives. You must have some magic formula about how to save these lives. What is it? We'd like to hear some concrete recommendations from you as to how we can reduce the number of accidents and fatalities. I don't know that we want to listen to your life story, even though it may be interesting."

"Have you seen my report?" I asked McAdams.

"No, I haven't," he answered.

"Do you intend to ask for it?"

"No, we do not."

"Doesn't your curiosity or concern for this subject lead you to want to see it so you can evaluate whether it has no value, some value, a lot of value, or whether it ought to be thrown in the wastebasket?"

"Well, Mr. Ryther, that report is an internal FAA matter, and I don't think the FAA would give it to us even if we asked for it."

"But have you asked?"

"No, I told you we hadn't."

"If you ask you might get it, or perhaps, as you say, you might be denied."

"Well, if we were denied, what good would it do us to have asked? Do you have a copy of the report?"

"I do."

"Well, Mr. Ryther, if you're the big private citizen which I understand you are, you ought to feel some responsibility for bringing this out to the American public and expose it."

"I will at the proper time and place. But as far as you are concerned, your source for the report is not me, but the government agency that has it. And that's the FAA and I most strongly urge you to ask them for it."

"Well, Mr. Ryther, it's their privilege if they wish to deny the release of the report. After all, you were in the government long enough to know that there is an age-old custom of executive privilege, and an executive agency doesn't have to release anything it doesn't want to release."

"But," I ventured, "wouldn't it be worthwhile to ask, and if you can't have it wouldn't you get some kind of insight into the FAA from knowing that you've been turned down?"

"Mr. Ryther, we have not asked for that report, and

we do not intend to ask for it. If you want to show us your copy we'll be happy to look at it."

At this point, Laurel looked at his wristwatch and said, "Well, I have another appointment, and I'm sorry, gentlemen, but I've got to run along." McAdams chose this moment to look at his wristwatch as well, and found that he, too, had another appointment. With handshakes all around they left.

At Admiral Thayer's bidding I remained behind a couple of minutes longer. "Mr. Ryther, I don't know how to apologize for Mr. McAdams's attitude. Frankly, I don't agree with him, I think this report should be made part of the public record."

"Naturally I agree with you, Admiral," I said. "In fact, it's my belief that the President under no circumstances would tolerate having one part of the executive department deny another part of the executive department access to its files if they were relevant or probably relevant to the subject the board is considering. I'm certain that if the President knew one department was withholding from another files that were relevant—especially to something like one of these awful plane crashes—that he would feel that was the poorest kind of administration."

Thayer agreed and we parted, but it wasn't the last I was to hear of the board.

Three weeks after my visit with the three members of the safety board, I received a telephone call from John Repasy, a Cincinnati businessman whose son had been a member of the Marshall University football team killed in the November plane crash. Repasy had read of me in *Look* magazine, and he had discussed the article with a group of parents who had lost sons in the crash. Repasy, who was representing the group, said they would be in Washington to attend the hearings that were being reopened because additional evidence had come to light at the end of June, and would I be willing to meet with them. I agreed and on June 22, I met with about thirty persons in the Skyline Inn, less than a mile south of the Capitol Building in Washington.

The dinner that followed the meeting was anything but happy. These people had only one thing on their minds: was there any more information about the accident that had taken the lives of members of their families. During and after dinner there was considerable discussion about me and my role in the FAA, and how the FAA operates.

At a strategy session after dinner they discussed the following day's activities. They had been told by the National Transportation Safety Board that none of them —not even a single representative—would be permitted to speak or ask questions at the hearing. The reason given by the board was that none of them had come forward in advance and presented sufficient evidence that they had knowledge about the accident. Not a single opportunity was to be permitted this group to ask any questions of the experts who were to appear before the board. As I've stated previously, this, in fact, is the way the board works. Consequently, only industry, government and aviation organizations usually get the opportunity to testify or to question witnesses. The general public, which the board apparently considers not worthy of taking part, is excluded from participation and permitted only to observe.

In defense of this policy, the board usually gives several reasons. It contends that it is interested only in the technical aspects of the accident under investigation, and therefore cannot be bothered by lawyers representing potential litigants in accident suits. The board is forever being contacted by these lawyers, who attend the hearing only for the purpose of acting as advocates for their side—planting questions and seeking answers that could aid their clients in lawsuits growing out of the accident. The NTSB reports are not by themselves admissible as evidence in civil court suits, and lawyers spend hours poring over transcripts of NTSB hearings to build their own cases.

In conducting itself in such a manner, however, the safety board is obviously not only discouraging public participation, but is shutting itself off from what could be a highly valuable source of new ideas and information.

The idea of actively excluding the public was nothing new to at least one member of the board— Francis H. McAdams, a former member of the CAB. It is widely known in Washington that the CAB, as well as the other major economic regulatory agencies—Interstate Commerce Commission, Federal Communications Commission, Federal Power Commission—has actively tried to keep the public out of regulatory hearings. These agencies, which claim to act in the public interest, are in actuality little more than arbiters of disputes between major corporations, each seeking economic gain for itself. With very few exceptions these agencies and their regular clientele—the airlines, broadcasters, railroads, truckers, bus lines, gas pipelines—have with regularity tried to shut out representatives of the public from taking part in regulatory proceedings. The courts, however, have gradually begun to break up this clubby relationship between the regulator and the regulated. Such an attitude, however, persists in great degree at the safety board.

Knowing the board's policy, the Marshall University group concluded that they were going to try to be heard anyway. They appointed Repasy chairman and instructed him to try to gain the attention of the chairman of the hearing and inform him that the group was there not to condemn the board or the government or make any claims against the government, but to express their interest and concern with what the government can do to prevent another accident like the Huntington one. They instructed him to ask the chairman why I had not been invited to testify either at the original hearing or at this reopened hearing, and request that my name be added to the docket as one of the expert witnesses.

These families advised Repasy that they wanted the board to consider the so-called double standard for certificated air carriers and charter aircraft. Under FAA rules the pilot of a certificated aircraft must have landed at a given airport within the previous sixty days before he is authorized to carry passengers into that airport. There is no such requirement for pilots of chartered planes. Although Southern Airways is a certificated carrier, its ill-fated flight into Huntington, West Virginia, that November night was considered a chartered flight, and it was the first time the pilot had landed at Huntington. The group felt very strongly that possibly the pilot's lack of knowledge of the surroundings of that airport had a bearing on the crash. So they were insistent on asking the government—through the NTSB—why there was this double standard for charter and scheduled flights.

The hearings were scheduled for 9:30 the following morning, June 23, in a hearing room within the block-square granite building in southwest Washington that houses the Department of Transportation. No sooner had Oscar Laurel, the acting chairman, arrived and gaveled the hearing to order, than John Repasy asked to be recognized. Repasy introduced himself and identified himself as representing the football team's families. The chairman ruled him out of order. Laurel said he would be happy to have the families remain at the hearing, but that Repasy was not on the docket as a witness or as anyone's representative, and that the board must proceed in accordance with the docket. Repasy, however, did not sit down. Staring at Laurel, and with a loud voioe, Repasy said, "Mr. Chairman, I apologize, but I insist on being heard. I insist that you and all others in this room see who we are." Then Repasy had each mother, father and widow attending stand and be introduced to the chairman—who did not interrupt them. Then, Repasy attempted to ask Laurel the first question that the group had decided upon—why I wasn't on the docket. But he was shut off and not permitted to speak again. Repasy made another attempt—this time to bring up the subject of the so-called double standard—but again Laurel gaveled him down.

On looking at the transcript of the hearing later, I found that none of this colloquy between Repasy and Laurel at the opening session was shown. A board official said that the stenographic reporter was late, and missed that part of the hearing. Repasy did, however, make it into the transcript of the afternoon session of the first day. It notes that during the questioning of one witness, an individual who is identified by the stenographic reporter as "an unidentified man," arose from the audience and started to ask a question, but was stopped in mid-sentence by Laurel: "Wait a minute. Wait a minute. I will not allow any kind of interruption in the orderly process of this hearing, sir, not from the floor. I told you from the very beginning we stand ready to respond to any questions that you might have when we have the time for it. Please, sir, we cannot, under any circumstances, allow any questions from the floor or any disturbances to take place. Now I will be happy to meet with you at any time to try to respond to whatever questions you may have in any particular area, sir. So we thank you, sir."

Thus is how the public is treated at National Transportation Safety Board hearings. The corporations and the airlines and the aviation establishment generally get a hearing, but the public is told its questions may be answered some day in private if somebody has time.

This, of course, does not mean that absolutely no member of the public is allowed to speak. If you happen to be a congressman you can usually get the floor and no NTSB hearing chairman would dare try to shut you off. Thus it was that two congressmen spoke during these hearings—Representative Ken Hechler (who once taught at Marshall University) and Representative James Kee, both West Virginia Democrats.

Hechler, who spoke briefly at the second day of the hearings, was critical of the board's procedures of not allowing representatives of the victims to testify or to question witnesses. He noted that the permanent chairman, John H. Reed, had written to a representative of the Marshall University parents and cited the board's rules concerning the lack of any special knowledge or aeronautical skills as the reason why this group was excluded from being a party to the hearing.

"I simply made this observation, Mr. Chairman," Hechler said, "that in other areas—and I cite particularly coal mine safety, one that I have been very closely engaged in—frequently those going around with the wheels and [who] are the so-called experts in a particular situation, frequently they do not have the freshness and independence of viewpoint which enables them to see and bring to the surface the basic facts which are necessary in order to reach sound, practical conclusions.

"It is for this reason that I feel that there is scarcely any group that has more special knowledge than those who have lost those that are close to them, than the group of which I speak."

Hechler said it was "unfortunate that the rules of procedure which have been established by the NTSB do not allow the participation of those interested parties. And I would like to conclude, Mr. Chairman, by expressing the strong hope that any and all questions which this group has should be entertained, answered, and fully explored by this board of inquiry."

Laurel made no comment. Nor did he after Kee spoke the following day and expressed his concern "about the feelings of the people who have lost their loved ones." Kee submitted a list of nearly a dozen questions to the safety board—including the question of the double standard and the intriguing question of why it was not made clear during the board's investigation that the FAA had not installed an instrument landing system at Huntington until after the fatal crash. Had there been another monumental snafu in the FAA supply system that delayed installation of the instrument system—and had, in fact, this delay resulted in the disaster that wiped out the Marshall University football team?

CHAPTER XXIV

AND FINALLY THE PRESIDENT

The lack of interest of the National Transportation Safety Board, the runaround I had received from the White House staff and the apparent indifference of just about everyone else in the government with whom I had spoken gnawed at me for weeks. Out of a sense of almost complete frustration I decided to address an appeal directly to the President. I realized, of course, that thousands of letters are addressed to the President daily and that few of them ever reach his desk. But I felt that in my case things would be different. After all, I was presenting him with evidence of the grossest nonfeasance in office which had taken place in his own Department of Transportation. How could he ignore such evidence, I reasoned.

My letter to President Richard M. Nixon was brief, a bit more than a page and a half, single-spaced:

"Dear Mr. President:

"Prior to leaving the Federal Service last December I had the privilege of heading a highly competent and ethical staff of aviation experts in the Federal Aviation Administration of the U.S. Department of Transportation.

"Over a year ago my staff and I submitted a report to FAA management which reflected many serious aviation safety problems together with thirty (30) recommendations for their solution. Our report gave special emphasis to the operation of charter flights and urged that immediate action be taken by FAA Management to correct the conditions we found. We warned that unless and until corrective action was taken the flying public would be in imminent danger. Months passed with no action taken by FAA officials.

"Almost six (6) months to the day after we submitted our report a charter flight crashed in Colorado killing thirty-one (31), including many members of the Wichita State University football team. About six (6) weeks after that another charter flight crashed at Huntington, West Virginia, killing seventy-five (75) including almost the entire Marshall University football team.

"Our report still has not been made available to the public and the acting chairman of the National Transportation Safety Board states that the FAA has not made it available to that Board. This Board is responsible for making the official determination of the probable cause of Civil Aviation accidents.

"Mr. President, I remember well how you expressed your personal concern for aviation safety last fall when the nation was shocked at the loss of these two university football teams.

"I have personally brought this subject to the attention of high officials on your White House staff as well as to top officials at FAA and the Department of Transportation. Not withstanding the series of aviation disasters in our country over the last few months, our reports and recommendations are still being covered up, effective steps have not been taken to correct the hazardous conditions which exist and the public is not being dealt with candidly and forthrightly by the federal officials responsible for aviation safety.

"I make the strongest recommendation to you that you replace the seven men in FAA and the Department of Transportation, where the key aviation safety responsibility is vested, with men of the highest competence, unquestioned integrity, and a strong will to correct existing conditions promptly.

"Another football season is on the horizon and aircraft charter arrangements are now being made by many colleges. I urge you to act so the nation may be spared another Wichita State or Marshall University disaster."

Once I completed the letter and signed it on July 9, 1971, I decided to call ahead to the White House to let at least somebody know it was coming. I called Peter Millspaugh and told him I'd written a letter to the President concerning my aviation safety report.

"Maybe you'd like me to bring it downtown and deliver it to you," I suggested.

"Oh Phil, today's Friday. If you'll just drop it in the mail I'll have it Monday," Millspaugh replied.

"Well, you've made the decision. But I think I ought to tell you further that at the same time I put the letter into the mailbox to the President I intend to release it to the press and selected members of Congress." (I sent copies to ten senators and half a dozen congressmen.)

"Oh, well, that's interesting. How long is it?"

"Not long."

"Could you read it to me?"

I read the letter.

"Well, well, well. Could you bring it down?" Millspaugh asked.

"Well, that's what I called you for—to suggest that I bring it down. But you decided to have it put into the mail. Now, do you want me to change that? You want to see it?"

"Oh yes, Phil. I want to see it right away."

I drove downtown and, after the usual problem finding a parking space in the White House area, I walked into the Seventeenth Street entrance of the Executive Office Building, a gray Victorian building with columns and balconies that once was used by the State, War and Navy departments. It adjoins the White House on the west. Inside, a uniformed officer at a desk pointed me toward a room on the first floor. I told the man at the counter there who I was and he said, "Oh, yes, we expected you. Would you sign right here and indicate what it is you are leaving with me," he said, proffering a document across the counter. I signed and he took the letter and gave it to a messenger. "This man here is waiting for it. He will deliver it now," I was told.

That was Friday. The following Wednesday Millspaugh telephoned me at my home during midafternoon.

"I wanted to tell you what has happened and what we're doing concerning your letter," Millspaugh said. "We've established a task force here to be chaired by John Dean [counsel to the President]. Other members of the staff will be on the task force, and its function will be to examine the entire matter discussed in your letter to the President.

"I want to say two other things to you as well. First, we have addressed your letter to Secretary Volpe at the Department of Transportation with a request that he prepare a reply to it and send it to the White House for signature. As soon as we receive it, we'll send it along to you—but we've said we want it answered here.

"Number two, the task force is requesting Mr. Volpe to provide a complete report to the White House on your report, the recommendations you made and what he has done about it, and it is our intention, Phil, that as soon as we get Mr. Volpe's report we would like to go over it with you so you can see it and comment on it."

I was really surprised. Apparently a letter to the President really can mean something. "That's fine, just fine." I told Millspaugh. "It looks as though somebody is genuinely going to get busy. I'll be leaving, incidentally, on a vacation in about two days and I'll be gone about five weeks. During that period naturally I'm out of circulation, but I gather from what you say that I can expect some mail when I return."

"You sure should have some," Millspaugh answered, and he wished me well on my vacation.

I returned nearly six weeks later, on August 23. Somewhat to my surprise (although by this time I should have been used to it) there was no letter from the White House awaiting me. On August 25 I again called Millspaugh and reminded him of our July conversation.

"You know, Phil, I've gotten out of this thing now, and I want to get back into it again because I'd like to know what's happened. I'll be back to you." And the following day he phoned. "You know, Phil, they've moved the whole task force function out from under John Dean and placed it directly in John Ehrlichman's hands, but I'll see if I can find out what's happened."

By this time my patience had worn thin; after all, it was nearly a year and a half since the completion of our report, and I had spent the better part of six months getting transferred from department to department and from White House desk to White House desk. So, in a moment of pique I said to Millspaugh, "Peter, why do you get yourself into the position that you're in. You've been promising, making commitments, but you never come through with anything." Millspaugh's voice turned chilly briefly, but he continued to assure me that he was doing the best he could, and he was going to find out what was going on.

During the discussion he mentioned that an assistant to Ehrlichman, Egil Krogh, Jr., was handling the matter personally.

I called Krogh later, but he was too busy to talk with me. He did find time to tell his secretary that he wasn't handling it any more, and that it had now been transferred to a Dr. Charles L. Clapp.

I called Dr. Clapp. But Dr. Clapp was occupied with a long-distance telephone call. He would call back, I was told. He never did.

So it was that even an appeal to the President failed to accomplish anything. It wasn't the end of the line— I did try elsewhere, and there were times later on when I achieved brief flashes of success in my attempt to make our government conscious of the problems of aviation safety.

But the work of much of my life was over. And since it's usually educational to reflect on the reasons why things went the way they did, I gave some thought to my experiences. I thought about each of the principal characters who affected my life during my last year with the FAA and in the months following my retirement to try to figure out what motives had impelled each to act as he had, why each had failed to make any significant move toward improving aviation safety and, in consequence, the safety of millions of individuals who fly as pilots or passengers.

There was Archie W. League, my boss. Archie failed to act, and in fact sat on my report, because any action would have resulted in offending his contemporaries who had shown him throughout his career that it was a good idea not to break step with the crowd.

Then there was Kenneth M. Smith, the FAA's deputy administrator, fresh in from private industry, who had heard about those lazy no-good civil servants. His aim was to correct the ills of government by chopping a few heads. Mine was the first.

And John H. Shaffer, the FAA administrator. He had been so badly burned by what amounted to the first strike in FAA history—a "sick-in" by flight controllers— and had sustained such severe congressional criticism, that he was determined to avoid further controversy. As a result, he was always away or "unavailable" when I tried to confront him with the failures of his agency. And James M. Beggs, undersecretary of Transportation and the man who actually ran the Department of Transportation. He knew of the quarrel within the FAA between those who wanted to improve it and those who wanted the status quo. But because of his own personal differences with top FAA officials, Beggs remained aloof from the internal squabble and allowed the FAA bureaucrats to settle things among themselves.

There was, of course, Senator James B. Pearson of Kansas. The senator had been profuse in expressing his sorrow and sympathy for the families that had suffered such great losses, but it was clear that he didn't want to press the matter of our report. Apparently it wasn't sufficiently important for him to anger the chairman of the Senate Commerce Aviation Subcommittee, Senator Howard W. Cannon of Nevada, whose attitude toward the aviation establishment over the years had been kind, cooperative and not always in the public interest.

And I could not forget folksy Ab Herman, executive assistant to the chairman of the Republican National Committee, Senator Robert J. Dole of Kansas. Dole's sole contribution to aviation safety was a memo to some staff official at the White House who declined to respond to the senator's inquiry.

And Peter Millspaugh at the White House talked a good game and expressed all the right emotions—horror, sorrow, shock. He gave his pledge several times to act, but never followed through. He seemed to promise most when faced with an immediate public relations crisis— the *Look* magazine article and my letter to the President which I said I was sending to several senators and selected newspapers. But when the heat died down, so did his enthusiasm.

And last there was the National Transportation Safety Board. Its failure even to try to obtain a copy of my report could be put down as sheer laziness. But it is entirely possible that the members feared they would not be reappointed if they appeared interested in challenging the FAA, a branch of the Department of Transportation. After all, the safety board itself is part of DOT.

The lesson of all this is clear enough. The bureaucracy, as led by political appointees, is unwilling to face up to undoing a poor performance. The bureaucrats themselves are afraid to do anything that will reflect unfavorably on their peers. Each overseer of the bureaucracy has his own reason for failing to act, but it generally amounts to keeping peace with those to whom he owes political favors, such as his own job.

And so it is that those very agencies that are supposed to be the staunch guardians of our safety—the agencies that were created to keep the air lanes safe for you and me—turn out to be little more than a single incredible bureaucracy. Incredible because it is a bureaucracy stalled by a lack of leadership—one that is frightened, ineffectual and reluctant to act. Its members are bound by political ties and past favors to those they regulate and to those to whom they owe their jobs.

The most unfortunate part of it all is that these political IOU's are never paid by those who borrowed the favors. They are paid by the public—and not in money, but in human lives.

APPENDIX

EVALUATION OF AVIATION SAFETY

CIVIL AVIATION U.S.A.

Popularly Known as the Ryther Report

March 30, 1970

This evaluation was made to determine the extent to which the Federal Aviation Administration is carrying out its assigned mission to promote safety of flight in civil aviation in air commerce. This evaluation did not include the aircraft management and flight inspection functions of the Flight Standards Service. These functions will be dealt with at a later date in a separate project.

The evaluation was conducted through extensive work with a wide range of industry, other pertinent government agencies, the journeyman inspector agency work force, and all levels of agency management.

Emphasis in this report was given to those areas which require agency management attention and decision. This report will not recite those areas which were found in good order; however, because of the significance and importance of air carrier operations, it is appropriate to indicate that, generally speaking, the Flight Standards Service surveillance and promotion of safety in the operations and maintenance of the certificated air carriers is in good shape.

The areas found to be in need of prompt attention which will be developed are:

    I. Federal Aviation Regulations.

    II. General Aviation Pilot Training.

    III. General Aviation Accident Prevention.

    IV. Experience Statistics Relating to Airmen, Aircraft, Accidents and Incidents.

    V. Surveillance of Airmen and Aircraft.

    VI. Violations and Enforcement.

    VII. Certificated Air Carriers, Air Taxis and Commercial Activities.

    VIII. Aircraft Manufacturing.

I. FEDERAL AVIATION REGULATIONS

Meetings with many industry and FAA people revealed a myriad of difficulties with the Federal Aviation Regulations. Primarily, these difficulties with the rules are:

1. They are not up to date.

2. They are unclear.

3. They are unenforceable.

4. The development time is too long.

5. Proposed rules are dropped because of industry political pressure.

We realize that all of the above conditions do not apply to all regulations, but they occur sufficiently often to place them in the "need fixing" category.

FAA regulations are subject to many different interpretations between regions in the areas of manufacturing, maintenance, and operations. As an example, applicants for a major alteration to an aircraft will shop between regions to locate the region that will approve the alteration in a subordinate field office. Some regions require the more complicated Supplemental Type Certificate (STC) for the alteration which requires the approval of the regional office itself.

The industry says that the attempt being made by FAA to clarify rules through the Advisory Circular (AC) method is just not fast enough.

Most persons within and external to the agency complain about the time required by the agency to adopt a rule. This is evidenced in part by a Flight Standards Service chart which depicts 325 days as a typical schedule for processing a simple, non-controversial rule requiring no public hearings. There are instances, and they are quite common, where rules have been in the rulemaking process for several years.

The industry complains that FAA rules have not kept up with technology. They say they expect some lag in areas such as jet engines, helicopters and the use of training simulators, but not a period of years. The effect on the manufacturing industry is one of creating delays. The effect on the air carriers is increased operating costs.

Many of our inspectors comment that we should be more forceful in the promulgation of rules. They say that rules which are required to enhance safety are proposed and then later withdrawn. Most FAA field offices and their inspectors believe that FAA allows itself to be swayed too much by a minority of dissent.

Many rules are not specific enough to be enforced.

Attempts to do so result in violation actions that are later dropped because of an inability to "prove" noncompliance. (This will be discussed further under Violations/Enforcement.)

Conclusions

Since FAA is primarily a regulatory agency in the field of airmen and aircraft certification, it is essential that the intent of the rules be clear and that the rules be up to date, expeditiously promulgated, and fully enforceable.

Too much credence has been placed in the past on that part of the Federal Aviation Act that specifies we should "foster aviation." Many proposed rule changes are met with the hue and cry that they will retard the advancement of aviation. FAA should adopt a strong resolution that any advancement to safety is a definite advancement of aviation.

FAA presently conducts some coordination meetings with industry in the rulemaking process; however, there is need for improvement. There is a definite need to formalize the process and to conduct these meetings annually.

Recommendations

1. Take immediate steps to establish formal annual review of the regulations. This should be a joint industry/FAA review and include representation of those:

    a. Who must operate under the rules,

    b. Who must surveil those who must operate under the rules, and

    c. Who must enforce these rules through violation proceedings.

This review should include a sufficient number of FAA and industry journeymen personnel to assure that the rules are workable.

2. As soon as the FAA/industry review is concluded, move to have the new regulation in effect promptly but in any event before the next annual review.

3. Take the necessary steps to assure uniform interpretation of regulations throughout the agency.

II. GENERAL AVIATION PILOT TRAINING

FAA is tolerating an unsafe condition in the area of general aviation pilot training; a condition which, unless corrected soon, will contribute to a further deterioration of safety.

Many general aviation pilots, particularly private pilots, do not have the judgment required to exercise the privileges of their certificates and consequently are a menace to themselves and others. Good judgment is acquired by training and experience. Lack of adequate training and/or lack of recent experience rate high as causes of general aviation accidents. As told to us, the attitude of many student pilots is to get a private certificate with the least possible effort and cost and "learn to fly later."

For years FAA field personnel responsible for surveilling this most important phase of aviation have been told that their prime functions are: (1) to promote safety and (2) to foster aviation. General Aviation District Offices (GADO's) have followed existing agency policy and have "fostered" aviation by allowing the quantity of flight schools to completely overshadow the need for quality.

As a result, GADO's have not been able to keep abreast of their main function, that of promoting safety.

Flight schools operate under either (or both) FAR [Federal Aviation Regulation] 141 or FAR 61. Those schools training pilots under FAR 141 are required to employ a chief flight instructor, meet certain floor space and equipment requirements, keep records, and have an approved curriculum. In exchange for meeting these requirements a flying school is certificated by the agency as "FAA approved" and allowed to publicize its certificate and to qualify a student pilot for a private pilot license in a minimum of 35 hours of flight time.

The vast majority of FAA Flight Standards personnel, flight school owners, operators and pilots believe that a student isn't adequately trained until he has acquired a minimum of 50 flight training hours. Even with 50 hours, this does not qualify a pilot to operate in a high density area. The theory which allows a pilot to do only those things for which he has been adequately trained is known as "training to proficiency," or training to a prescribed skill level, and is subscribed to by almost 100 percent of those to whom we talked.

The minimum requirement of 35 hours, as presently specified in the regulations, was all right in the 1940's but in the last 20 years both the aircraft and the environment in which they operate have become much more complex. The fact that many students now qualify for a private pilot certificate with the minimum number of flight hours indicates that the qualifying flight examinations are obsolete and too easy.

Many "FAA approved" flight schools which try to deal in quality training of student pilots soon find that they cannot compete with Part 61 operators or Part 141 operators who qualify student pilots in 35 or 40 hours of flight time. If it were not for the Veterans Administration's requirement to approve "GI training" only at FAA approved schools which have been in operation for at least two years, most Part 141 operators would be conducting training under Part 61 to avoid record-keeping requirements and resultant FAA surveillance. We are told that unless FAA raises its standards for flight schools, many "quality" operators will be forced to operate in an "unsafe manner" in order to meet competition.

General Aviation District Office (GADO) personnel state that ground schools, both FAA approved and otherwise, are considerably deficient. Many "FAA approved" flight schools claim that there is no money in ground schools because any "fly-by-night" operator can *guarantee* an applicant passing his written examination. GADO's estimated that 90 percent of applicants know the questions on the written exam before they take it.

GADO's report that there are too many flight instructors and a substantial number are of questionable quality. The turnover rate of flight instructors at most flight schools is tremendous. Most are relatively young men who are trying to build up their total flight hours to the point where they can get a job with an airline or air taxi operator. Many flight instructors are good pilots but poor instructors. FAA exorcises very little control over the quality of this instruction. Under the present regulations, FAA cannot prohibit an operator from conducting a flight school regardless of how bad the teaching practices might be. If it is an "FAA approved" school, the agency can only revoke the certificate, in which case the school is free to operate as nonapproved.

Recommendations

1. Flight training be accomplished only by FAA approved flight schools; the requirements of such schools is to be upgraded to insure that only quality enterprises gain FAA approved status. The upgraded requirements should provide the same standard for a small school with 3 aircraft and 5 students, as is prescribed for the large school with 50 aircraft and 300 students. Also, by having only "FAA approved" schools the agency retains the authority to control the quality of training wherever it is done.

2. Ground schools not be allowed to operate as a separate entity, but should be an integral part of FAA approved flight schools.

3. The vehicle used to upgrade the quality of FAA approved schools should adopt the concept of "training to proficiency" with 50 hours as a minimum flight time requirement for private pilots.

4. Develop (or have developed) standard curricula for all pilot training. These curricula, along with lesson plans, should be provided by the agency to FAA approved flying schools to assure uniform training. Industry should be invited to participate in this effort.

5. Raise the flight test and written examination standards for both the private pilot and the flight instructor commensurate with the new training requirements.

6. Develop, distribute and require the use of a standard record-keeping system (with standard forms) at approved flying schools.

7. Flight instructors be required to complete a flight instructor course given at an FAA approved school for initial certification. Employment at an FAA approved flight school should be a prerequisite to recertification.

III. GENERAL AVIATION ACCIDENT PREVENTION

The Accident Prevention Specialist Program which is being conducted under a test condition in the Central and Southwest regions has been in progress for approximately two years. The purpose of the program is to reduce general aviation accidents. As a means to accomplish this, an Accident Prevention Specialist is assigned to each general aviation district. The specialist is given broad guidelines to develop and use any techniques that he feels will be effective in reducing accidents. After a two-year test period, the efforts in each general aviation district in both regions have settled down to one pattern. Generally speaking, each Accident Prevention Specialist conducts safety seminars. At these seminars, movies are shown and lectures are given concerning different facets of safety. In addition, many publications are developed by these specialists and distributed to the flying public. At the all day safety seminars, the Accident Prevention Specialist gives check rides to general aviation pilots who wish to have their proficiency monitored without fear of violation action. Both regions have developed a Counselor Program. These Counselors are experienced aviation-minded individuals who make their time available for counseling purposes to all airmen who want help.

Interviews with FAA and non-FAA people, and analysis of the statistics related to the Accident Prevention Specialist Program, have led to five conclusions:

1. The FAA cannot actually determine the exact value of the program. The number of accidents per thousand hours have been too rough a gauge with which to determine trends over the short run of the test period. Also, the definition of reportable accidents was changed on 1 January 1968 and has made measurement of 1968 and 1969 accident statistics against previous experience invalid. A month-by-month analysis of the statistics indicates some reduction of aviation accidents in the two test regions.

2. The program has improved the public image of the agency. Many private pilots who have attended the seminars and counseling sessions said they now see the FAA, for the first time, attempting to assist the individual pilots to be safer.

3. Many suggested the program would have been more successful if:

a. The specialist's efforts could have been directed to the half dozen most significant causes of accidents.

b. The specialist had been given an accurate inventory of all the aircraft and airmen in his district.

4. Since participation by general aviation is voluntary, only safety minded pilots attend the meetings and receive the benefits of the program. The pilots that would benefit most from the program are not attending and participating.

5. The Accident Prevention Specialist Program alone is not accomplishing the FAA mission of reducing accidents. More must be done by the FAA in other general aviation areas in concert with the program. The FAA

must upgrade the training of airmen, not only by improving the quality of flight schools but more importantly by improving the quality of flight instructors. Several general aviation districts have begun giving all flight instructors check rides and have increased surveillance of their work. These General Aviation District Offices have reported up to a 50 percent reduction in aircraft accidents. The inspectors must spend more time in the field, especially on weekends and at uncontrolled airports. When these inspectors are in the field they must be conspicuous to the pilots and be zealous in pursuing violators. The image of the inspector must be that of a law enforcement officer. With this image will come improved compliance with regulations and it will improve aviation safety and reduce accidents.

Recommendations

1. The Accident Prevention Specialist Program be adopted nationally and put into effect by 1 July 1970.

2. Weekend and holiday surveillance at busy uncontrolled airports be substantially increased. The work schedule of the inspectors be arranged to provide maximum surveillance on weekends and holidays at all locations.

IV. EXPERIENCE STATISTICS RELATING TO AIRMEN, AIRCRAFT, ACCIDENTS AND INCIDENTS

The agency has not done a good job in determining what meaningful data it needs in surveilling civil aircraft and airmen in the interest of reducing accidents and incidents.

Industry generally derives little benefit from aircraft

population and aircraft maintenance data which the agency collects at Oklahoma City. The inspector work force is not provided meaningful data concerning the underlying root reasons why airmen are involved in accidents. In this connection, it is believed we learn very little that will be helpful in taking corrective action when we merely know that the cause of the accident was "pilot error." For example, we need to know more about the pilot's training and recent experience background and the relationship of the aircraft to the accident. At the present time, the agency is involved in "rehashing" the approach we have been using for many years with respect to experience data gathering and analysis.

Key management people at the Aeronautical Center were unanimous in stating the agency has not objectively determined what kinds of data it needs and they made the strongest recommendation that such determination be made promptly.

Recommendations

1. The agency take a fresh look and determine what will be really meaningful in the way of statistics and how they will be used in better surveilling aircraft manufacturers, aircraft and airmen population to reduce accidents and incidents.

2. The agency should retain the services of a private firm with extensive background in the statistics and data field to assist with this effort.

V. SURVEILLANCE OF AIRMEN AND AIRCRAFT

There are more than 500,000 pilots in the United States. Qualifications of these pilots range from the airline pilot with thousands of hours of flying time to the private pilot who may have only 35 hours of flying time and has just received his FAA certificate. Seventy thousand new student pilots enter the system each year. More than 100,000 mechanics are employed in maintaining the 125,000 active aircraft. These men and machines are certificated by the FAA and subject to either continuous or periodic surveillance by safety inspectors. To surveil this tremendous number of men and machines, Flight Standards Service employs a "firing line" inspector force of approximately 1,400 men.

Approximately one half of the 1,400-man inspector force employees in the so-called "firing line" positions are assigned to general aviation. These 700 inspectors, maintenance and operations, have the responsibility for certification, recertification and surveillance of all airmen and aircraft other than air carrier.

A primary function of these inspectors is to promote safety—that is, to prevent accidents. A great number of general aviation accidents are attributable to pilot error. Pilot errors result from poor or inadequate training, lack of proficiency, or poor judgment. Under present regulations training is the only one of these which can be directly influenced by surveillance by the general aviation inspector.

It would then seem appropriate that surveillance of airmen training should be placed high on the inspector's list of priorities. However, under present practice he is unable to do this. Approximately 50 percent of his time is spent in administration and non-safety related tasks. Additionally, the inspector is told that accident investigation, air taxi surveillance and the processing of violations must take precedence over basic surveillance of pilot training. As a consequence a very small part of his time is spent in assuring that pilots are being adequately trained and properly tested for the certificates which the FAA issues to them.

Inspector personnel are almost unanimous in their statements that flight instructors are inadequately trained, poorly motivated, inexperienced and only engaged in flight instruction as a means to an end—that is, accumulating the time necessary to qualify for a better paying job. Many are therefore temporary in nature, and ineffective as teachers. The lack of adequate surveillance over this large and vital segment of those persons responsible for the training of pilots is considered to be a major weakness in the general aviation surveillance function.

The investigation and processing of violations is a time-consuming and unrewarding task, and it is in this area that the inspector has a feeling of futility. The regulations are often vague, difficult to interpret and even harder to enforce. An inspector seeking to complete a violation action against an airman faces an uphill battle all the way. After having to furnish proof for every statement he makes through every level of the process he gets the feeling that his integrity is on trial rather than that of the violator.

The processing of violations is cumbersome and time-consuming. It is not unusual for an inspector to devote weeks to processing a violation action against a flagrant and repeating violator. Even if he is successful in substantiating a violation, the agency's policy is to slap the wrist of the violator rather than levy a meaningful penalty.

An inspector should be able to "cite" a violator as easily and effectively as a state traffic officer issues a ticket for speeding.

All non-air carrier aircraft must be inspected for airworthiness at least annually. The authority to conduct these inspections is delegated to authorized inspectors (AI's). These delegations must be made to all applicants who qualify. Surveillance of these AI's, who number in the thousands, is cursory at best, especially in remote locations. Many FAA inspectors state that some AI's issue Airworthiness Certificates without performing the necessary inspections. AI delegations are renewed automatically on the 31st of each March to those who have complied with the basic activity requirements. Adequate surveillance of the manner in which these designees conduct business for the FAA is often difficult since there is no requirement that they have a fixed base of operations.

Records of inspection bearing the AI's number displayed prominently on the aircraft, similar to the system used on automobiles, would make surveillance of this vital function much easier, resulting in a savings in man-hours and safer aircraft.

In an attempt to increase the efficiency of the surveillance function of inspectors, Flight Standards Service has formed permanent inspection teams called Systemsworthiness Analysis Programs (SWAP) teams.

The SWAP concept as a technique to monitor both air carrier and general aviation is sound. The idea of surveilling to determine the "systemsworthiness" of an operator is the proper role of the U. S. Government. It was found that our SWAP teams are not performing as it was intended but have in many cases lapsed into nitpicking. Selection of team membership has not been sound. Training and supervision of the teams has been weak and an air of a contest has arisen between SWAP teams and the principal inspectors. The SWAP function has a temporary or ad hoc connotation as expressed by FAA personnel both in the regional and district offices.

Recommendations

1. Airmen Certification Inspectors be designated in the GADO's. The job functions of these specialists be confined solely to surveillance of flying schools, flight instructors, designated pilot examiners, and the flight checking of pilot appliances.

2. Enforcement specialists be assigned to each region and in larger field offices as necessary. Their function will be to investigate and process airmen violations in their entirety.

3. Violation reporting be simplified by providing that an inspector may issue a citation to an alleged violator with a copy to an enforcement specialist for further handling.

4. Every civil aircraft subject to annual inspection bear a record of that inspection displayed so that it is easily discernible and bearing the certificate number of the inspector.

5. The FAA completely review the SWAP function with particular attention on:

a. Organization location of the SWAP function both at headquarters and the field.

b. Team membership selection criteria by pay scales.

c. Relationship between the SWAP team and the "principal inspectors."

d. Whether the SWAP audit should concern itself with "systemsworthiness" or with detailed processes.

6. Amend FAR 65 to provide that the agency appoint Authorized Inspectors (AI's) on an "as needed" basis rather than the present provision that all qualified applications are entitled to an inspection authorization. The amended rule should also provide that an AI's authorization expire when he moves from the jurisdiction of the GADO which appointed him.

VI. VIOLATIONS AND ENFORCEMENT

FAA enforcement of regulations is inconsistent in general aviation, ranging anywhere from adequate to non-existent because the regulations are often too vague to be understood and interpreted uniformly by our inspectors and the public. As a result, it is difficult, if not impossible, for our inspectors and lawyers to effectively complete many enforcement cases.

The processing of a violation normally involves a review by Flight Standards management and general counsel at area and regional levels. In some locations, the time required for these reviews is lengthy. This factor, in the eyes of our inspectors and some of the airmen, tends to dilute the effectiveness of the enforcement action.

The distribution of GADO's and the number of inspectors assigned to each office has a significant bearing on the enforcement coverage throughout the country. The airports at or near the GADO get better surveillance and consequently more enforcement than those in the remote areas of a district. It may be argued that little or no surveillance is needed in these remote areas since aviation is not as big. However, airmen and airport managers in these areas are concerned about the frequent and willful violations taking place. While a small percentage of the airmen (pilots and mechanics) are responsible for the violations, their actions affect everyone's safety.

Recommendations

1. In the development of new or the revision of current regulations, FAA should pay particular attention to the enforceability of each part. (Is the intent clear, is it understandable to both airmen and inspector, does it convey the same meaning to both, and can the inspector readily determine when a violation occurs?)

2. The FAA inspector be the sole authority needed for support of enforcement cases. Statements from others should not be required when an FAA inspector witnessed the violation. The inspector's authority should be clearly spelled out.

3. The processing of enforcement cases should be substantially speeded up. Multiple levels of review should be minimized.

4. Violations be entered on an airman's certificate in the same manner as traffic violations are entered on drivers' licenses in some states.

VII. CERTIFICATED AIR CARRIERS, AIR TAXIS AND COMMERCIAL ACTIVITIES

The certificated air carriers, which include the supplementals and commercial operators, are relatively well organized and operate in accordance with the guidelines contained in FAR 121.

In recent years, the tremendous growth of air taxis has brought out serious safety problems, pointing out the need for better regulation. Air taxis now operate under the provisions of FAR 135. Since the agency has recently made extensive amendments to this part of the regulations which will become effective 1 April 1970, it was not considered appropriate to fully evaluate air taxis until after that date.

Many inspectors are concerned over their inability to properly control or surveil the activities of noncertificated operators. These operators engage in the commercial transportation of passengers and cargo under the very minimal requirements of FAR Part 91. Qualifications of crews and mechanics employed by many of these operators are marginal, and inspectors, in an attempt to improve the safety of these operators, often devote an inordinate amount of time to this surveillance. Some inspectors have resorted to appealing to the better judgment of "customers" in attempting to dissuade them from doing business with operators who they feel operate in a potentially hazardous manner. These operations are particularly prevalent in the lucrative Caribbean and South American trade.

Recommendations

1. Upgrade the regulations governing "noncertificated" (Part 91) operators to provide stricter controls over all phases of their operations.

2. Intensify surveillance and enforcement to keep pace with this segment of aviation.

3. Evaluate the effectiveness of the new air taxi regulation, FAR 135, after it has been in effect a reasonable period of time.

VIII. AIRCRAFT MANUFACTURING

In recent years major airplane manufacturers have made wide use of subcontractors and component producers which FAA does not adequately surveil. FAA has attempted to expand its engineering/inspection coverage, but we have been unable to "keep up," even though the agency has enlisted the help of industry by appointing company personnel as "designated" government representatives. Some manufacturers that build light aircraft operate under delegated option authority (DOA), and have been given wide latitude in the self-surveillance of design, manufacturing and quality control of their products. Companies producing large transport aircraft are not given DOA; however, FAA assigns engineering and inspection responsibilities to individuals within the company. Our evaluation revealed the following significant deficiencies.

DOA manufacturers are surveilled too infrequently to assure compliance with airworthiness regulations and DOA procedures. The regional surveillance teams are inconsistent in their surveillance coverage and deficiency follow-up and sometimes the findings get a "nit-picking" connotation. Also, the time that elapses between surveillance efforts invites relaxation of the quality control efforts of the companies.

There are numerous checks that FAA could delegate to industry, but has not. Manufacturers requiring engineering or inspection approval by FAA often experience considerable delays and red tape. The delays occur primarily because of FAA's heavy workload, and the physical separation between our regional/district offices and the manufacturers.

One region indicated we would not have designees, if FAA had time to perform the checks themselves. This thinking is outmoded and FAA should prove their faith in industry by granting additional delegation of authority.

Industry pointed out that many of their engineers are involved in basic research. They indicate that every time they develop new design concepts or make a technological breakthrough they must spend considerable time training and convincing FAA engineers that the new concepts are valid. However, there is no indication that industry desires FAA to pull out. They suggest that FAA redirect some of their effort from the "routine, tried and proven items" to those matters involving new technology that are not covered by current regulations.

Recommendations

1. Surveillance of DOA manufacturers should be conducted by FAA at more frequent intervals and more concentration be given to the quality control practices of the manufacturers. To insure uniformity, a centralized surveillance team should operate across regional lines and cover all DOA manufacturers.

2. Delegate additional engineering/inspection authority to industry to minimize delays resulting from the "back and forth" with government offices. Designated Engineering Representatives and Designated Manufacturing Inspection Representatives be appointed at manufacturing plants that produce subsystems, avionics, and other aircraft components.

3. Determine those engineering and manufacturing

matters which are critical to producing a safe aircraft. The efforts of FAA field personnel should then be redirected to concentrate on these important matters.

4. Identify new technology in aircraft manufacturing that is not covered by current regulations and develop guidelines, policies and regulations to govern these new engineering innovations.